PRIZE FIGHTER

MAINSTREAM SPORT

PRIZE FIGHTER

THE LIFE AND TIMES OF BOB FITZSIMMONS

DALE WEBB

MAINSTREAM
PUBLISHING

EDINBURGH AND LONDON

FOR CHRISTINE AND SOPHIE

First published in Great Britain in 2000 by
MAINSTREAM PUBLISHING COMPANY (EDINBURGH) LTD
7 Albany Street
Edinburgh EH1 3UG

This edition 2001

ISBN 1 84018 494 9

A catalogue record for this book is available from the British Library

Typeset in Plantin
Printed and bound in Great Britain by
Cox & Wyman Ltd

Contents

Acknowledgements

Additional research: Kent Upshon, Alec Webb, Richard Wallis, Martin Matthews, Bill Matthews, Eric Bradshaw, Gary and Barbara Sparta (New Jersey, USA), Linda Parkhurst (Sydney, Australia), Joe Cataio (Chicago, USA), the late Gilbert Odd, Robert Davies and boxing historians, past and present.

Representation by David O Leary Literary Agents, London.

Photography by Jeremy Postle.

And special thanks to Colin and Marlene for their continued support — I told you it would be alright on the day . . .

Prologue

Shouting, singing, laughing, joking, talking. Lively, boisterous crowds densely packing the sun-bleached, dusty pavements, cramped spaces thick with bodies, slow queues zig-zagging here and there. The air hanging heavy with noise and humidity, the crowded mass of humanity adding to the clammy, claustrophobic atmosphere. A tangible buzz surrounded them, drawing them together as one. Men sleeping in doorways, the result of overbooked guest-houses. Families queuing for food and drink, hungry with anticipation. All around them, others are laying bets, exchanging odds, giving advice, arguing points.

For weeks the sports pages had preached the advent of this particular gospel. Those lucky enough to be here could consider themselves at the front of a queue which stretched around the world. Tonight, the eyes of the world were on the events in this American town; events which would inflame into a full-blown action spectacular that would light up the night skies, events which would be faithfully re-created in painstaking blow-by-blow detail across the headlines of tomorrow s newspapers.

This was entertainment.

It is said that in film or television, violence is controlled and sanitised. Slowed down and cleaned up. A physical fight is seen as an act of grace and movement, presented in a choreographed form with a beginning, a middle and an end. An actor punches another a dozen times; only a bruise or a slight cut in sight.

A shake of the head is enough to bring the victim back to full consciousness, in order to once more resume the staged ballet. A man left for dead will arise, rubbing his head and dusting himself off, as he climbs to his feet. It s part of the performance, being played out within unwritten rules. We expect it. We demand it. We want to see the bad guy get his come-uppance. We want to see the good guy exert his physical and moral superiority.

It s in this way that violence has been edited and packaged, in order to become an accepted part of our daily entertainment.

This is theatre.

Here, the real thing was being unleashed in a confined space: a deadly uncontrollable force materialising, as if an all-powerful demon had been conjured up. Here, there is no control, no pressure-valve, no escape. The actions were in double-quick time; independent and simultaneous. When the punches landed, they landed with a nauseating crunch, tearing flesh and cracking bone. Again and again the force was enough to snap a man s head back. Both attacked at once, in a syncopated flurry of blurred arms and spattered blood. Anger gave a white-hot urgency to the blows; while skill added an ice-cool potency to their aim.

As the two gladiators ungracefully embraced — an involuntary gesture borne of desperate fatigue — the threat from each was cancelled out. As they were drawn apart by the shirt-sleeved referee, the irregular rhythm of flying fists resumed once more, with only mounting tiredness pulling the punches and cushioning their darting blows. Once more, they embraced in a tangled sweaty mass. Once more the immediate threat was equally neutralised.

Beyond them, beyond the dirt-packed roped square in which they performed, deafening cheers and shouts of encouragement blurred into white noise. Whipped up into ever-higher levels of sheer excitement, the fifteen thousand people cramming the area beyond the ring screamed for more. The pitch of their cries rose and fell in relation to the intensity of the fighting. A lull would bring low groans; renewed attacks would cause the fervour to surge.

For those close, each punch could be heard to draw a gasp from the recipient, as he rallied against the shock and pain. The first few rows could sense brutal power being generated, raw force being spent. Every hammer-blow was accompanied by a chorus of winces from ring-side seats, as shock waves generated far beyond the thrashing pair. Each strike was capable of killing a normal man, each block was desperately staving off lethal injury.

This was real life.

The time of change can be traced back to the year 1889. The events of that day would mark a passing of one age to another: the birth of a sport from the death of an age-old tradition. The men of that time have passed into history, both in body and in spirit. Either way, they are no more.

The exact location of this momentous event was the town of Richburg, Mississippi. It took place in the clearing of an obscure wooded area, beneath the glare of a blisteringly hot sun. Two men, bare-chested and bare-fisted, stood facing each other within a twenty-four-foot square which had been roped off. Around them were gathered several thousand spectators, many clad in smart hats and coats despite the overbearing humidity. They were crowded together in uncomfortable rows, peering over heads and shoulders, craning for a better view.

The two men were one John Sullivan and one Jake Kilrain — heavyset, well-muscled warriors with powerful arms and huge, broad shoulders. Both were experienced and well-versed in this form of contest.

According to the London Prize Ring Rules, the two would enter into a fight with the winner being the only one left standing. Ten thousand dollars were at stake for the winner, along with the title of the World Heavyweight Prizefighting Championship. A well-dressed gentleman in the middle of the square — the referee — was a man named John Fitzpatrick, who would, in later years, be elected as Mayor of New Orleans. A heavily-moustached man, standing menacingly nearby to ensure fair play, could be identified as Black Bat Masterson, formerly a lawman of the notorious Dodge City. In addition, extra security was provided by Captain Tom Jamieson and his Mississippi Rangers, who patrolled the crowd with loaded Winchester rifles.

As the battle commenced, all eyes immediately fixed on the thrashing bare limbs tangling in the centre of the sun-bleached ring.

In years to come eye-witness descriptions would describe the men clashing repeatedly, raw fists hammering relentlessly on unprotected heads as the strength of each took its bloody toll on the other. The contest would last for seventy-five rounds; a total of two hours and sixteen minutes of fighting. It would only end when Kilrain could no longer stand and his corner called for the match to be stopped. The referee took pity on the injured man and named Sullivan as the winner.

This would be the last world championship title fight to be fought with bare-knuckles. This marked a turning point which saw the gutter trade of the illegal prizefight transformed into the sport we know today as boxing. Many would see such a fight as a spectacle of brutality.

For the two men this was prize fighting. And this was their world.

1. Champion of the World

Helston, Cornwall
October 1999

Since the Iron Age, a settlement has existed near the far southern
coast of West Cornwall, standing guard at the gateway to the
jagged Lizard Peninsula. It s from here that wildly dramatic
seascapes stretch out into the dark, foreboding depths of the
Atlantic Ocean, the gateway to the United States of America.

A Domesday Book entry of 1068 describes this very settlement
as the manor of Henlistn. Henlistn would later become Helston, a
coinage town which formed a focal point for the large-scale trading
and mining which would shape Cornwall and its economy. Tin
ingots mined across the county would be taken there to be weighed
and valued. The duty payable to the Duke of Cornwall was assessed
from this, as traders bought and sold the metal which
geographically and financially underpinned the Duchy.

Helston was once a port at the head of the River Cober, which
silted up in the 13th century, leaving behind the Loe lake on the
Penrose Estate. The main thoroughfare through the town, the
aptly-named Coinagehall Street, is the venue for an annual festival
which takes place on 8 May every year. The Furry Dance — when
couples dressed in their Sunday best dance in a loose formation
through the streets — has become a well-known date in the
calendars of both tourists and locals.

But tonight, the town looked as if it was about to turn in.
Workers spilled out of office buildings, in search of cars and buses,
to wind their weary way home. The air of finality which marks the
end of the working week was evident, as traffic began to trail
towards the town s rainswept outskirts.

On this bitterly cold evening, the wintry weather lent a matt-grey shade to the buildings and streets. People scurried along the glistening pavements, bound up for protection in bulky coats and anoraks. A stream of cars stopped and started, as the traffic lights guided their slow progress. Headlights pointed the way ahead, casting poles of light along the darkening street. Doors swung to and fro, as shoppers laden with bags ventured out from brightly lit stores into the damp descending gloom. Faces scowled as the ice-cold wind cut into them; heads bowed, away from the worst of the blasts. An everyday winter scene in an everyday town, on the verge of the twenty-first century.

The first clue to our story — one which will forever be associated with Helston s past — lay on the exterior of an average-sized pub on the right-hand side. The Fitzsimmons Arms threw a welcoming light through the falling dusk. The sign swinging above the always open door bore a hand-painted image which hinted at a local tale of folklore. The painting on the sign showed an artist s impression of a balding, bare-chested man. As people scurried below it, the sightless eyes gazed blankly out across the street.

Behind this image lies a colourful tale — one of the most remarkable ever heard. But it s not an example of the legends which entwine the history of this romantic corner of Britain. This story is true. It s an adventure story which took its leading character to the other side of the world, far from this scene of normality, to a time and place in history which was anything but normal. Set against a backdrop of wild frontiers and conquering heroes, it s a story of fame, success and notoriety — one man s journey to the top of the mountain.

Further along the road, past the traffic lights in the town centre, lay the second clue to our pilgrimage. A small blue china plaque on one of the terraced cottages confirmed the near-biblical legend which has been handed down through generations of Cornish schoolboys. It s a legend of how a local boy, born in this street, became one of the most famous men of his generation, achieving this fame in a far-off land, among the cowboys, gamblers and sportsmen of an era well-known to movie-goers across the world.

> BORN HERE, 1863. ROBERT FITZSIMMONS, CHAMPION OF
> THE WORLD, 1897.

CHAMPION OF THE WORLD

The story which lies behind the words on that plaque is one of heroes and villains, glory and greed in the far-off countries of New Zealand, Australia and the United States of America — parts of the world which were still relatively untamed.

It s here that a fascinating assortment of carefully-preserved relics summon up an age long since past — a collection of faded posters, boasting of attractions too good to miss. The talk is of betting and form, of fighters and fighting. These were the early days of sporting endeavour — acts of heroism played out on a foreign stage, as yet unblighted by the onset of television or radio commercialism, and yet already tainted by the hungry way in which heroes were consumed in an art which demanded all, yet returned comparatively little to all but the very few.

The yellowing pages of long-preserved newspapers date from a time when cowboys really did fight Indians, and a good part of America was still a vast, undiscovered wilderness. In an age of frontiers and settlers, one man was well on his way to becoming one of the most celebrated figures of that far-off era. In a culture completely alien to that which we know today, he stood head and shoulders above mere mortals, catapulted to infamy by the sheer force of his all-conquering personality and electrifying life-force.

His followers were of the less-than-genteel variety. (The phrase rough-and-ready could be deemed rather more appropriate.) During one particular title-fight, more than three hundred sidearms were confiscated from the crowd as they filed in to the arena. They were collected by one of the West s most notorious gunmen, who d been put in charge of the event s security. In a time when the cult of celebrity hadn t yet been invented, the star of the show dominated both the front and back pages of newspapers from Brisbane to Birmingham, with his professional and personal dramas vying with each other for the public s attention. In doing so, he was gloriously politically incorrect, living life with a cheerfully self-destructive disregard which would later characterise the sport he helped nurture through its infant years.

This was the man who enjoyed such nicknames as Lanky Bob , Ruby Robert , the Cornishman , the Blacksmith , Rock Cod and the Kangaroo . He was paid a king s ransom, and yet he made you feel that he deserved it; indeed, that he had been born to it. He was married to a total of four very beautiful women and yet his own countenance could, at best, be described as lived-in . He enjoyed life to the very full, draining the last drop of the metaphorical vat of good living, while constantly and greedily demanding more. Taking a perverse pleasure in squandering the equivalent of millions of pounds on the lifestyle of a king, he went to the very edge in pursuit of his dreams. He became a legend, a legend created from a man named Robert Fitzsimmons.

And here in his home town, eighty-three years after his death, they still talk about him.

If there is a story behind the legend; it follows that there is also a man behind the story. This is a point at which many a hero has let down his public, when his seeming immortality is fractured by human frailty. We are often bitterly disappointed when we find our idol has feet of clay.

With his spindly legs in their specially-padded tights, and his stiff-backed, rather awkward gait, the Cornish prodigy was seen as an oddity among the hulking bruisers who dominated the noble art of prizefighting during the late nineteenth century. The word art is not to be taken lightly, with masterful skill and reflexes called upon repeatedly during brutal contests which sometimes lasted for up to seven agonising hours and a hundred gruelling rounds. Fitzsimmons was often mocked for his vivid red hair, abundance of freckles and skinny frame. As such he was was also the subject of much merriment. However, the merriment often ceased when he swung into action, for he could easily stun a man into senselessness with one extraordinary punch in the heat of a full-blown fight.

When we examine his story closely, we find that so many romantic notions surround the man s illustrious career that it is difficult to separate truth from fiction, especially with regard to the actual extent of his abilities and his supposed physical shortcomings. In truth, the Cornish-born former blacksmith was neither a monster nor a freak. In fact, he was a slightly-built man of average height — in his prime he weighed only around 165 pounds. His look was characterised by his highly-freckled pale skin, and a rapidly-thinning crop of bright red hair. He was far from a swashbuckling Adonis — he possessed wild, slightly bulging eyes and a stern, rather fierce expression. Although his arms and shoulders were typically those of the burly mineworkers from his native land, his lower half looked likely to buckle at any moment under the uneven weight. But he held no fear in hand-to-hand combat, taking on a never-ending succession of giant bruisers without the slightest hesitation, dispatching them to the canvas with a highly-skilful combination of quicksilver speed, instant reflexes and an almighty punch. He coined the famous phrase, The bigger they are, the harder they fall and it s one he lived by; thrilling packed audiences with a series of David-and-Goliath-style fighting displays.

Robert Fitzsimmons was far from being a cold-blooded thug. From the start of his rousting career, he brought a healthy dose of unashamedly flamboyant showmanship to what had been a dour, hard-faced spectacle: a spectacle in which men were often beaten to within an inch of their lives. Using his wiry athleticism and natural grace, he was able to move fast when occasion demanded, but was also prone to showboating — prancing around the ring in order to show off to an appreciative crowd. It was in this way that he injected a much-needed shot of vitality and a long-overdue dash of colour to the sport which would soon become an American obsession. An irrepressible joker, a childish mischief-maker, a lovable rogue — all of these descriptions have been applied to the man who would become the heavyweight champion of the world, and if they don t completely sum up his larger-than-life character, they certainly go some way to explaining the many legions of fans who would travel for days to see him in action. When he took to the ring, a show was in store in which literally anything could happen. While some athletes plot their movements based on tactics and planning, Fitzsimmons was the sort of man who would either overcome any challenge before him, or kill himself trying. In short, he was just the sort of personality that boxing needed, in order to develop from a sleazy, dangerous bar-room diversion into the socially accepted spectator sport it was to become in later years.

In a career of just over thirty years — he continued prizefighting until he was finally refused a licence at the grand old age of 53 —

Fitzsimmons claimed to have just under 370 contests. While this may be taken with a rather delicate pinch of salt, as the great man was often prone to bouts of wild exaggeration, the fact remains, however, that his record and achievements are unlikely to be equalled. He is still the smallest man ever to win the world heavyweight title, and was the first to win world titles at three different weights. In later years, regardless of age catching up with him, he insisted that he was capable of taking on any man, anywhere, with the gloves on.

In his glorious prime, he was an invincible, unstoppable force, darting across the ring with an uncanny grace, hitting with unbelievable velocity from any angle or direction. He could punch harder and faster than any before him. At the height of his powers, stunned opponents fell lifelessly at his feet as if they d been pole-axed. Even if they glimpsed the killer blow coming, they were usually powerless to stop it. When he was elevated to the prestigious inner circle of the noble art, he proved he was worthy of such illustrious company, disrespectfully inflicting a series of comprehensive beatings on some of the best fighters in the world. In a series of spectacular upsets, he soundly knocked the reigning kings of the prize ring headlong from their thrones, overthrowing the greatest names of the era, from Nonpareil Jack Dempsey to Sailor Tom Sharkey. Each round was a battle, and each bout was a war, with no quarter given, expected, or received.

Fitzsimmons s heroic contests ranged from a 90-second knockout victory in an illegal prizefight staged on an open prairie near the American-Mexican border, to epic long-distance heavyweight contests before huge arenas bursting with thousands of fans. At his peak, he was in danger of running out of opponents, such was his all-encompassing domination. A series of travelling roadshows saw him take on the local talent from whichever area he and his entourage happened to be passing through. It was by this means that the great public of the United States were able to witness close-up the pace and skill required for a fighter to become a top champion. Those who were foolhardy enough to step into the ring to take him on for a couple of rounds were given a painful lesson in fighting they wouldn t forget. The biggest, meanest labourers, mineworkers and cowboys from coast to coast were soundly knocked out by the humble Cornish blacksmith who was fast becoming an international celebrity. Fitz — as he was fondly known to all — was once described by a leading sportswriter of the day, as possessing prestige, craft . . . and a wallop that s the greatest in all the world. A man absolutely without fear . . . he is the gamest and most dangerous man the ring ever saw . . . at close range he is the greatest fighter the world ever knew.

The Englishman s career had also brought him to the attention of the authorities on more than one occasion; when police were called in to break up illicit fights, which were staged against strict state laws in dingy, decrepit backstreet halls and other secret locations. Although prizefighting had officially existed in America since 1816, when Jacob Hyer and Tom Beasley famously fought a competitive bare-knuckled bout in New York, it was thought by the largely puritanical society to be the lowest, coarsest form of crude entertainment, watched only by the underbelly of society — tramps, vagrants and criminals. In audience terms they may actually have had something of a point — the majority of early fights were often staged in the ramshackle back-rooms of illegal drinking dens or disreputable taverns, especially in areas popular with sailors who d come across the Atlantic from England, where competitive fighting had already gained a loyal following. Contests in those days often pitted home-grown American boys against Irish immigrants, with rowdy support for both sides in the more keenly-fought matches. These would have been deadly, no-holds-barred affairs, with few rules or regulations to hamper what was essentially an old-fashioned streetfight. From this time until well into the next century, the top echelon of the fighting elite would be dominated by the Irish. Men such as Jim Corbett, John Sullivan and Jack Dempsey, emanating from good Irish stock, who would rise from the murky depths of the pursuit to become household names.

The proud exception to this was Fitzsimmons, who d come all the way from Cornwall via New Zealand and Australia. This often left the US audiences in some doubt as to whether he should be backed or barracked, as was the dilemma when he fought Jim Corbett in front of a home crowd on St Patrick s Day. Fitzsimmons always thought of himself as a true Cornishman — a feeling which was no doubt shared by the huge crowds of miners from that celebrated county who packed the rowdy audiences at his fights, cheering him on with a patriotic pride which would have added an extra sting to his performances. When this particular fighter climbed into the ring, an expectant thrill would have run through the waiting crowd. You would have been guaranteed an action-packed bill; as he would either club his opponent to the ground almost immediately or engage in such a bloody battle that one of them was sure to go down. And stay down.

The actual power contained in his mighty fists was phenomenal; many a hulking opponent was reduced to a breathless heap and on the receiving end of a particularly keen wallop . In later years, when he assumed the role of the sport s elder statesman, living the life of a well-to-do gentleman, his hands and face would bear the lasting scars of a hundred battles. This was a man who epitomised the hard, often brutal sport of prizefighting, and, what s more, was more than happy to do so. It s said neighbours in the well-heeled suburb of New York where he eventually bought a mansion were alarmed to discover that a man who earned his living with his fists was intending to put down roots among their professional numbers. As usual however, his winning personality triumphed — rather than being disgusted by a coarse street thug, they were said to have been extremely taken by the charming gentleman and his lovely wife and family. In getting to that house, Fitzsimmons had fought his way to a life of fame and riches — the like of which he could never have dreamed of, all those years ago, as he beat horseshoes into shape. Social commentators poured accolades on him, proclaiming him as an excellent ambassador for his field of endeavour. Here was a truly remarkable man, living in a truly remarkable time.

Fitzsimmons the fighter was virtually unrivalled; but Fitzsimmons the entertainer was in a league of his own. It was when he launched a devastating attack on an opponent that the entire crowd would hold its collective breath, their attention totally captivated by the performer he undoubtedly was. Practically inventing the image of a sporting superstar, every aspect of his life was geared to entertaining the public, whether it was in a boxing ring, on the variety stage or presenting to the world the larger-than-life persona which ensured his place in the celebrity gossip columns as well as the sporting pages. Some of his most bizarre showbiz stunts were often seen during periods of intensive training. These sessions often involved lengthy runs, violent sparring bouts and agonising work-outs. As if all this weren t enough, the boxer could often be found in the cage of Nero, his pet lion. Charging spectators twenty-five cents a head to witness these unorthodox playfights, Fitzsimmons was simply playing up to his public persona. And putting on a show. When he stepped outside the ring, his life was equally — if not even more — colourful. His womanising ways included the seduction of his manager s sister, who would later become his second wife. Ironically, his manager then married Bob s ex-wife, which must have led to some lively get-togethers at Thanksgiving.

Bob Fitzsimmons was instrumental in the development of the sport, speaking out strongly on the dangers of bare-knuckle fighting and unlimited rounds and helping to banish them as relics of the past. He was keen to give something back to the pursuit which had given him so much.

It was as a result of his efforts that he received a letter in 1905 from none other than President Theodore Roosevelt, wishing him the compliments of the Christmas season. Although the boxer refused to elaborate on the exact contents of the letter, he admitted it had been sent from the White House. The fact was reported in the *New York Times* of 30 December, 1905. Another report from Washington has Roosevelt once referring to the fighter as my dear friend, Bob . He was also immortalised in marble by the sculptor Gutzon Borgium. Borgium — who famously created the presidential busts at Mount Rushmore in South Dakota — is quoted as saying: He is one of the best specimens of manhood in the world. He possesses lines built for the sculptor to work upon. His muscles are clean-cut and long. His neck is so short that he can almost draw his head down even with his shoulders. Few of the statues of the ancient gladiators show physiques equal to that of Fitzsimmons.

PRIZE FIGHTER

Bob Fitzsimmons will be remembered for the legacy he left for future generations of boxing. In an age when boxers lives hung in the balance, Fitzsimmons not only survived but prospered. He not only won; he won in style.

2. Family Ties

Helston, Cornwall
26 May 1863

At the time of Fitzsimmons s birth, Cornwall was enduring a turbulent time; in both economic and personal terms.

Since the advent of civilisation, the county of Cornwall — a rugged land of singularly dramatic beauty, lying on the southwest corner of England — had been famed for its tin mining. Since Phoenician times, men had extracted ore from the ground with local skills and resources that ranked among the best in the Western world. It was an industry which could trace its roots back some four thousand years. But now, in the latter half of the nineteenth century, times were changing. Cheaper overseas production had indirectly led to one of the biggest movements of people ever known in the civilised world. Miners were moving overseas to find work which was being denied them in their homeland. Eventually, many of them would have no choice — emigrate, or starve. Another theory has also been advanced, following further study of the emigration patterns of the Cornish race. This suggests that mass emigration actually pre-dated Cornwall s de-industrialisation by around thirty years, with an emigration trade already emerging in the county by that time, facilitating lucrative new lives abroad, for those armed with the skills — and the will — to make their way on the other side of the world. Either way, the county formed one of the most significant emigration bases in Europe, with Cornishmen apparently being more than three times as likely to leave than their counterparts elsewhere in Britain. The trend really gathered pace during the 1840s with people heading to North America — the favoured destination — along with Australia, South Africa and South America.

PRIZE FIGHTER

The Cornish inventor Richard Trevithick — credited with inventing the steam engine — is said to have lived for a while in South America during the early 1820s. Doubtless he wasn t the first of his countrymen to go there, and he certainly wasn t the last. Cornish emigrants have also been traced in New South Wales blazing a trail for the voyages to come. A report on the welfare of Cornish miners in 1904 would reveal that as many as 64 per cent had worked abroad — often in more than one country. It seems, however, that they didn t absorb themselves totally into their new cultures. Proudly protecting their Cornish identity, they would set up ex-pat communities — a home from home. It was this pattern of emigration that led to the proliferation of Cousin Jacks — transplanted Cornish miners — in the furthest corners of the globe. Their descendants can still be found there today; as the saying goes, Wherever there s a hole in the ground, you re likely to find a Cornishman at the bottom of it. While miners had never been particularly well-paid, the gradual loss during the late nineteenth century of the industry which had characterised the county for so long was a bitter blow to a proud, hard-working race, and continued to spur an ever-increasing exodus of men and women. Boats packed with miners and their families set sail from ports across Britain throughout this time, with the occupants undoubtedly anxious to start their new lives.

The passage to the other side of the world, the geographical scale of which could scarcely be contemplated by most making the voyage, would have been an experience both frightening and physically harrowing to even the most hardened of mineworkers. Conditions on the ships crammed with migr s were terrible; with disease, hunger and exhaustion decimating the crammed decks of waifs and urchins. Christened fever ships , they were a route to a new life, away from the hardship and misery which had characterised the lean years of the Cornish tin industry. A large ship would have carried between seven and eight hundred emigrants.

So, there was a chance to start a new life on the other side of the world, where opportunity beckoned and new horizons were forming. The stream of families upping sticks may have provided an inspiration for those who suddenly found themselves without work.

A local appeal for men to become police officers in a district of New Zealand eventually caught the eye of one James Fitzsimmons, and, it seems, history was made. James Fitzsimmons senior, who hailed from Omagh in County Tyrone, had served in the British Army and had also learned the trade of a blacksmith — the calling to which Robert and his brother, Jarrett, would also be drawn. James would later pave the way for his sons livelihoods by setting up in business as a veterinary blacksmith in New Zealand, his police career apparently abandoned. Jarrett, as the older of the pair, was something of a role model for young Robert. Stocky and strong, he was said to have been a noted Cornish wrestler; with his brawny build in contrast to his sibling s slight form.

The boys mother, formerly Jane Strongman, came from a Cornish family who lived in Truro. Bob once described her as a kind soul, who helped families nearby at a time when the disease of smallpox was rife in Cornwall. Records show Mrs Fitzsimmons was a midwife, working in the Helston district. Bob remembered her helping local families come to terms with the plague which claimed many lives at that time among the elderly and the young. His boyhood recollections also recount that the Fitzsimmons family wouldn t go untouched by tragedy. Henry, who would have been Bob s older brother — born in 1857 — died at the age of nine. Mrs Fitzsimmons was a religious woman, who harboured a desire to see her youngest son join the ministry. We can detect a certain cynicism on his part, however, as he once told a newspaper that his mother believed everything she read in the Bible . Competing for her attention with his eleven siblings, the young boy is said to have been outwardly agreeable to this future vocation, until he discovered that his true talents lay elsewhere.

Certainly, it must have been the furthest thing from Mrs Fitzsimmons s mind, as she held her infant son in her arms: this tiny, under-sized mite would one day become world heavyweight boxing champion.

Those young boys around Helston with whom Robert had engaged in rough play would almost certainly have been glad to see the back of him when his family emigrated, for he is said by local historians to have gained quite a reputation in a series of robust playground fights, even at such a comparatively tender age. He s described by those who knew him as being small for his age, with a mass of freckles and an unruly mop of hair. Even then, he was described as being lively and boisterous — a term which when applied to young boys usually translates as a handful of trouble .

The faction of the Fitzsimmons family who made the journey to New Zealand were venturing into the unknown as it s unlikely any of them had left Cornwall prior to this. Unknown to them, they d chosen a destination which enjoyed a natural beauty and a number of dramatic landscapes; similar to those of their homeland. From the South Canterbury coastline, the Timaru district of New Zealand spans over 2,600 square kilometres of the most diverse land imaginable. Green pasture, rolling hills and clear rivers form the character of the district, lying at the foot of New Zealand s spectacular Southern Alps. Its north and south boundaries are defined by two rivers, the Pareora and the Rangitata, both famed for their swimming and fishing. A particularly dramatic stretch of landscape lies in the north-westerly corner of Timaru district, running sixty-four kilometres beyond the Rangitata Gorge to Mesopotamia Station, in the high country. It was sparsely populated until around 1859, when the English ship *Strathalian* docked there with more than a hundred immigrants on board. Today, Timaru is renowned as a popular tourist destination boasting a population of around 42,000, famed for local produce such as *Canna* lilies. Back in the 1870s, however, it was still finding its feet, both socially and economically. It was to this district that the young Fitzsimmons would find himself billeted, having left his native Helston. His family quickly settled in to a new way of life and it was here that he spent his youth. It was here that he would discover the special talent that set him apart from other boys. Then his adventures would really begin.

The boy s steel-tipped boots clanked along the flagstones of the pavement as he cheerfully made his way home. He ambled along, in that meandering, aimless way which is unique to small boys. He looked around him, nodding to people he knew. Despite his casual manner, he was walking with an imagined sense of purpose, for he was on an errand for his mother. As such, the mission carried a great importance, with a severe penalty for fouling up. Young Robert Fitzsimmons was a lively-natured boy, constantly full of mischief, and his eyes twinkled brightly as he walked the narrow streets — a familar figure to the people of his native town. This was a time when young children were seen and not heard, and a clip round the ear from a policeman was apparently sufficient to maintain law and order among the youth. So it was that a boy of his age could be trusted to make the journey unaccompanied. He crossed the road, and entered the park at the edge of town, continuing on his route home. In the corner of his eye, he could just about make out a group of teenagers playing football. Shouts and jeers carried across the still air, as they continued their game.

His face froze as he realised a large, threatening youth was heading towards him. Eyes wide with fright, he froze to the spot, as the bigger boy strode towards him furiously. Robert tried to back away, looking around desperately for a means of escape. But the open grassland offered neither exit nor hiding place. He looked back at the aggressor, who was now looming large in his sights — a terrifying demon bearing down.

Robert didn t know what he d done to upset him — he d kicked the football back to the group in order to be helpful — just as the boy was running to fetch it. The player had obviously taken his wasted journey to heart and was planning to seek immediate vengeance. In his over-enthusiastic attempt to please, it seemed Robert had committed a grave error of judgement — one which was about to be painfully realised. Fists bunched by his sides, he came to a decision. He d tough it out — fight back. Chin set with resolve he looked up only for a large, bony fist to slam into his young face with a resounding crack. He screamed as his nose broke amid a gushing flow of blood. As his head whipped around under the force of the blow, his body began to lose consciousness. He was face down as he hit the ground. He sprawled into the mud and then lay still. The boy s inert body lay spreadeagled where he d fallen. His face was deathly pale. A mess of blood congealed across his mouth and nose where he d been hit. He looked like the victim of a road accident. As passers-by began to approach him, there was no sign of movement from the prostrate form. When he eventually came to, paralysed by pain and shock, he was surrounded by a crowd of concerned onlookers. A Good Samaritan had taken it upon himself to bathe his battered face, which helped to bring him back to consciousness. It was a miracle that he was still alive, having avoided choking on his own blood.

Describing the brutal attack in detail years later, Fitzsimmons said: I was so pleased with the opportunity of kicking the ball back to the players that I hadn t noticed the six-foot tall captain running himself after it. He was evidently displeased at his wasted energies. It was a classic case of being in the wrong place at the wrong time, and as any small boy will tell you, your options are limited in such a situation. An askew glance and a puffed-up male ego; the two can coincide with disastrous results. For a lively young lad, the shock would have been as bad as the physical injury.

Worse was to follow. When Mrs Fitzsimmons eventually got her hands on her son, she was furious. In keeping with her Christianity, she d repeatedly warned him not to get involved in fights. She put him across her knee and gave him a severe beating with a whip — his second assault within as many hours. The boy was sent to bed, a disconsolate, broken spirit, mortified with the unfairness of it all. It was only in the light of the next morning, when the eleven-year-old s face had swollen unrecognisably from his injury, that she realised her mistake. Filled with remorse, Mrs Fitzsimmons threw her arms round her son, sobbing with him, as he winced with pain.
 Right then and there I determined to prepare myself to settle scores with that big coward, who had not only broken my nose, but had been the means of securing such a humiliation at the hands of my mother, Fitzsimmons later related. The incident shocked him sufficiently to force a re-think of his career plans, abandoning the idea of joining the ministry. He visited church twice a week, singing in the choir, and also attended Bible classes. Now he had a new goal. From that day on, my sole desire was to become a prizefighter, and some day take satisfaction out of the giant who had handed me the sleeping potion at such an early age, he pronounced, rather dramatically.

It was around that time that the young boy visited his elder brother s blacksmiths, where he found two old aprons and stuffed them with shavings to make a roughly-hewn set of boxing gloves. From then on, young Robert practised his new trade as keenly as any new apprentice, taking part in youthful sparring exhibitions with boys from the neighbourhood. He s said to have borrowed large, hardened turnips from his mother s larder with which to hone his skills and toughen his young fists. His quicksilver hands, even at such a young age, would slam into the swinging turnips with considerable force, smashing them into pieces. By the age of fifteen, he would be taking part in competitive prizefights, where he showed a speed and dexterity which would immediately mark him out from the herd. Clearly, this boy was going places, and it was his turnip-prepared fists which would take him there.

As for that soccer captain it was perhaps fortunate for him that he was never seen again, despite young Robert s efforts in tracing him. The youth may never have discovered that the young boy he punched so viciously would go on to be one of the greatest fighters of all time. If he did, it s likely the thought would have caused him to break out into something of a cold sweat.

Later in his career, the boxer actually reflected that he had a lot to thank his attacker for, suggesting that it was his cowardly bullying which transformed a would-be blacksmith into a potential world champion. If it hadn t been for him, I would still be earning a few shillings per day at the forge, he laughed. Fitzsimmons recounted this episode in an article for *Boxing* magazine in 1913, (which is said to have been reprinted from an earlier edition of the *New York Herald*) titled, with typically subtle humour, How I Missed Being A Sky Pilot!

In it, he elaborated on the tale, saying part of the reason that his mother had been so angry was that he d lost the coin she d given him to buy some snuff, as it had flown out of his hand when he d been hit! He also says in the article that his face was swollen so badly that he was unable to go to church that weekend, but was made to go to school on the following Monday. This, it seemed, would spell the end of his educational career, at the age of eleven. The scholars laughed at me so much that I ran home and never went to another school or church ever again, he wrote. My mother used to send me to church, but I d lay on the grass outside and listen to the hymns, because I loved singing. Then I d ask someone what the text had been, so I could tell my mother when she asked after I had got home.

The serene backdrop of his local church was also the setting for another incident involving the young Robert, this time in an argument over a prayer book.

In a conversation recounted by the journalist and biographer Robert Davies, Fitzsimmons apparently remembered entering a poetry-reciting contest. His rival in this was the son of the preacher, with the prize of a gold-embossed prayer book on offer. The two boys recited poems by memory, one after the other, until the other boy began frantically racking his brains to remember any more. Always competive by nature, young Fitzsimmons took great pride in reciting his last poem, therefore winning the prize. Unfortunately, it seemed the preacher was not above a touch of nepotism. He gave his own son the book anyway. The undeserving prizewinner s erstwhile opponent took umbrage at this, and when the preacher s son emerged from the church, Bob was waiting for him. After a confrontation which no doubt involved a lively discussion about the rules of poetry contests, a fight ensued. The other boy was bigger and heavier than Fitzsimmons, but despite this advantage, two solid punches from the smaller adversary stopped him in his tracks, whereapon he turned and ran into the vestry, with Fitz in hot pursuit.

A final punch sent the bigger lad flying, and Bob escaped with the prayer book that he considered was rightfully his. He claimed to have learnt an important lesson of life from the episode, although it certainly wasn t one which would have been found in the pages of the aforementioned book: It was right there that I discovered what a sock I had, and that . . . is how I became a prizefighter.

After leaving school the youngest member of the Fitzsimmons clan helped out in the blacksmith s which had been established by his father, and would be passed on to his brother Jarrett. Predictably, such a relatively mundane profession wasn t sufficient to satisfy Bob s boundless lust for life; he dreamed of something bigger and better, beyond the confines of his home town. While practising his boxing skills, he worked as a carriage painter, executing the fine striping on the bodywork. This, too, didn t carry nearly enough mystique; so he then got a job as a striker in a local foundry, where he built up his upper-body muscles, swinging a huge sledge-hammer. Once more, though, his combustible temper got the better of him, and he was eventually sacked, having thrown a hot tyre at the foreman. It was while he was working at the foundry that he had his first competitive bareknuckle fight, at the age of fifteen. In the meantime, he earned his keep by working as a painter and then as a paper-hanger.

Eventually, he came back to work for his brother at the forge. He would stay there for the next five years, as his spare-time hobby began to develop into something rather more serious . . .

The eighteen-year-old youth could certainly have been forgiven for losing his nerve, such was the awesome vision which loomed terrifyingly before him. Never before had he peered so precariously over the very precipice of disaster. Facing him was the scourge of the local prize-fighting circuit, the awesome Timaru Terror , a freakishly-sized individual whose sheer bulk gave him an air of invincibility, which filled the dirt square cleared by the crowd. He was the sort of man who d scare the living daylights out of you if you ran into him on a dark night. In this part of New Zealand the Terror was feared and respected in equal amounts by those who followed the noble art in its raw form. A bully in every sense of the word, he would have been looking forward to punishing the impudence of the young upstart who d dared to invade his private domain. It would be an all-out brawl, with precious few rules for the faint-hearted to hide behind. Not that anyone with a vaguely faint heart would be here in the first place. The only rule where Terror was concerned was simply to stay out of his way, if at all possible. But for young Bob Fitzsimmons, it was too late for that. The athletic young apprentice blacksmith from Helston, Cornwall, was facing the greatest test of his life — a life which could conceivably be cut severely short in the next few moments.

History, of course, would relate a rather different story. The

PRIZE FIGHTER

Timaru Terror — an outsized blacksmith who usually went by the rather less intimidating name of Tom Baines — may himself have been forgiven for failing to take seriously the challenge from the skinny, ginger-haired teenager in front of him. A certain amount of arrogant, professional pride would have puffed his chest as he, the seasoned fight veteran, proudly made his way to the centre of the ring, menacingly raising his fists against the freckled, pasty newcomer. The next few moments, however, would change the course of sporting history — forever. Not only would Baines fail to terrorise the gangly youth, but he would receive the most vicious beating of his life, reeling from agonising punches to the face, eventually sprawling on the floor in a haze of pain and confusion. He was knocked unconscious inside of one round with the deceptively potent young Cornishman proving himself more than worthy of the task. A slow-burning fuse had proved to be a deadly time-bomb, which had blown up in the older man s face. A flame had been ignited that day, which would burn over the next three decades. That mighty feat may have been taken by some to be a fluke, but Fitz cast serious doubt on that half-baked theory when he later appeared in a boxing tournament organised by the British prizefighting champion, Jem Mace. Mace would go on to play an important part in Fitzsimmons s development as one of the world s greatest all-time fighters, but the boxer-turned-promoter couldn t have dreamed that the undersized middleweight he met out in New Zealand would have been capable of even defending himself in the ring, let alone contesting a championship.

Mace himself had been one of Britain s early prizefighting heroes, and was well-known for advocating the use of gloves — a practice which would later also be adopted by both Fitzsimmons and the famous John L Sullivan. Prior to Mace s day, protagonists — clad only in breeches and boots — would do battle in a squared-off ring of grass or dirt, before a cheering horde of top-hatted English gentlefolk, who would whoop and cry with delight when the first of the men drew blood with his fists.

Born in Norfolk, England, on 8 April 1831, Mace graduated from the fairground boxing booth where all comers would be invited to put on the gloves in the hope of lasting a few rounds. He went on to win the British middleweight crown, before stopping Sam Hurst in fifty minutes to become Heavyweight Champion of Great Britain. He was later recognised as the unofficial world heavyweight champion, defeating Joe Goss in one hour and forty-five minutes in 1863 — the year of Fitzsimmons s birth. There was another coincidence linking the two men — all of Mace s three brothers had been blacksmiths. In the year of 1880, Mace s boxing show was touring the Antipodes, taking on all comers with its robust stable of stars. Weighing only 140 pounds at the time, the seventeen-year-old Fitzsimmons would unwittingly cause a major upset to the show s smooth progress. Audiences would have been stunned into silence as the teenager knocked out four fully-grown men in cold blood, one after another. According to records, this feat actually earned him the unofficial title of Lightweight Champion of New Zealand. More importantly, spectators later said that they d never seen anyone hit so hard, fast, and with such deadly accuracy and execution. However, it seems lessons weren t learned. A year later, Mace was touring New Zealand with another show, this time showcasing the young hopeful Herbert Slade, a huge Maori who was being tipped as a future heavyweight champion. Fitzsimmons inflicted the biggest upset and hit him repeatedly with such force that the fight had to be stopped in the second round. Mace, the former champion, was so incensed by this disrespectful treatment of his valuable investment that he squared up to Fitzsimmons, before the two were hurriedly pulled apart. It s perhaps fortunate for the forty-nine-year-old veteran that they were.

The fact that prizefighting was frowned upon by much of decent society in those days made it necessary for the young Cornishman to hide his light under a bushel, at least for the time being: I had to go direct from my blacksmith s forge to the scene of battle, always living in fear that if my employer, or his foreman, should learn of what I was doing in my spare hours, I might, in consequence, be swelling the ranks of the unemployed. While the heavy physical work at the forge was undoubtedly building up his upper-body strength, it must have required a considerable effort to crawl out of bed on the morning after a fight to drag his battered body into work, as if he d spent the previous evening in pursuit of some respectable activity. As well as the dangers of his employers finding out what he was doing, there was also the possibility that a serious injury sustained in the ring would put paid to his day job.

As his reputation grew, first in New Zealand and later when he would move to Australia, Fitzsimmons developed from being the underdog to become the man to beat. Fighters from further and further afield would hear of his growing list of victims, and volunteer to meet him in the ring in the hope they d be the one to stop this advancing train. One of these men went by the name of Dick Ellis — a huge, brawny specimen who had comprehensively flattened every fighter who had been unfortunate enough to be pitted against him. Caring little for footwork, parrying or tactics, Ellis simply took the direct route — battering a man to within an inch of his life in the shortest time possible. If this approach wouldn t win any prizes for artistic content, it certainly appealed to crowds, who were guaranteed a ritual slaughter every time he stepped up before them. Fitzsimmons would look back on his fight with Ellis as one of his most popular contests. He claimed:

> Our fight was a rip-snorting affair . . . neither of us wasted any time with fancy footwork. It was simply a case of slug and repeat from start to finish, but it was exactly the sort of contest to please the crowd. There was very little science about it, as it was mostly a question of the ability of both of us to take punishment and wear down our opponent with a combination of in-fighting and hard, swift punches.

In the sternest test of his career so far, Fitzsimmons is said to have given his all in scrapping with this worthy opponent, with both men bleeding heavily from cuts to the face by the start of the second round. Every nerve, every sinew was tested to its limits as the street-brawl careered around the ring, with blows raining on either fighter s face and head. Never one to decry his own talents, Fitzsimmons claimed that it was only his steely determination and supreme physical fitness which began to see him overtaking his rival. Years later, he remembered: Ellis seemed to be running out of steam. He was breathing heavily . . . He could not stand the pace, and finally I landed on his jaw and body in just as rapid succession as my hands could move, and down and out he went. Battered but unbowed, the young Cornishman had apparently proved himself in the fiercest of competitions, dishing out the punishment while absorbing all that could be thrown at him.

There is, however, another side to this particular episode. So often in Fitzsimmons s life-story, fact merges with fiction, truth mixes with legend; and this is one such point where the edges become slightly blurred. Fitzsimmons gave the above account of the fight in a newspaper article in the early 1900s. His recollection of the event seems startlingly clear. But a later book of his ring career, *The Fighting Blacksmith* by Gilbert Odd, suggests that this contest never actually took place. It was supposed to have been staged on 17 December 1889 at a hall in Sydney. The event was billed as the championship of New Zealand, as both men had arrived on those shores from that country. In fact, it seems likely that the promoters of this bout were actually Ellis and Fitzsimmons themselves, for it was they who had hired the hall and advertised the forthcoming attraction. The venture was a disaster, as fewer than fifty tickets were sold, and the pair decided to bow out of the promoting business and cut their losses. So it would seem the fight never actually happened.

Unless there was another, unrecorded fight, it s possible that Fitzsimmons s memory may have been playing tricks with him, or that he thought it wise to draw a veil over this ill-fated enterprise.

Nevertheless, Fitz felt he was well and truly on his way now, beyond local fame, beyond back-street prizefights, to a world of glamour and glitz, fights and cash. Unfortunately, as so often happens in a sport which is sold on dreams, this failed to materialise. In simple terms, no-one in the Australian boxing community really took Fitzsimmons seriously, although they acknowledged his durability and punching power. It s likely that the spasmodic nature of his appearances, coupled with the fact that boxing didn t really receive a great deal of press at the time, meant that he wasn t given the kind of exposure which would have fuelled his career. During his seven years in Australia, he notched up just over twenty fights, many of which were classed as exhibition bouts, rather than championship material. But like young apprentices in industries all over the world, the Cornishman had to learn his craft. The raw material was there; his power and speed were not in doubt, but it had to be shaped, controlled and honed in order to become a complete athlete. There is a huge gulf between a brawler and a champion, and the young Fitzsimmons was learning his trade from the bottom up. With each fight, another part of the equation would have fallen into place, as he learned ring-craft, stealth, stamina and tactics.

It was soon clear to him, though, that to find his place in boxing s elite, he would have to travel rather further afield.

3. The Noble Art

In ancient Rome and Greece, competitions were regularly staged between two fit young men, whereupon they would wrap studded leather thongs around their fists and engage in a physical fight. In those fights the maximum possible injury was inflicted on one s opponent. This primitive form of prizefighting formed an important part of holiday celebrations and and often attracted huge crowds. The fights often only ended when one of the men was killed. This rather bloodthirsty entertainment continued until the years immediately prior to the Christian era, when one particular Roman emperor is said to have banned all such types of fist-fighting. As such, the first version of the sport which would later be known as boxing subsequently disappeared from view.

It was during the early part of the eighteenth century that the so-called noble art was fully revived in Britain. The pursuit really came to the fore in 1719, when a man named James Figg was acknowledged as the first national heavyweight champion. Figg later opened his own amphitheatre, where he staged exhibitions and lessons of pugilistic skill; attracting audiences of well-to-do sporting gentleman from across the country. Equally at ease with the fencing sword, Figg would later become generally recognised as the father of boxing . Following his death in 1740, the championship was assumed by one of his pupils, George Taylor. Taylor in turn was eventually followed by Jack Broughton, who established the boxing rules, inventing as he did the first codes of conduct in 1745, and the boxing glove, which was only used in sparring exhibitions. In 1838, the official London Prize Ring Rules were adopted, which loosely governed the competitive conduct of those men who took each other on, using either bare-knuckles or the scant protection of skintight leather gloves. Contests lasted until one man was physically incapable of continuing. Hitting a fallen opponent was outlawed, but in truth, by the time a man hit the floor, the damage had usually been done. The impact on a man s skull from a solid blow would almost certainly have led to serious injury in many cases and blood would flow freely in most bouts.

Aside from the physical hazards, prizefighting soon earned a highly disreputable image in English society. The sport would become a by-word for crooked double-dealing, as an often brutal pursuit was made all the more unpalatable to many, due to fixed fights, illegal punches, bribes and a whole host of other sins. Prints which still exist of early exchanges show bare-chested men squaring up to each other in roped-off grass rings, before a crowd of gentlemen , doubtless many of whom had varying amounts of money resting on the outcome. Illustrated images of bruised, battered and badly-cut fighters give us an idea of the punishment which would have been inflicted. Noses would be mashed into pulp, ears would be torn and permanent scarring or disfigurement suffered, as men beat each other into senselessness, in the spirit of all-out competition. For certain spectators, it was undoubtedly part of the attraction, but it was never publicly tolerated, remaining strictly illegal in most cities.

When prizefighting later reached America, largely due to sailors travelling across the Atlantic, bareknuckle bouts tended to be staged in out-of-the-way warehouses, barns or woods, in order to avoid being broken up by the police, with the participants then being arrested. As it had in Britain, the pursuit attracted a lot of criticism from certain sections of the American public, who felt that such events were both immoral and highly dangerous. A lack of supervision meant these fights were largely unfettered by rules or regulations, with gouging, butting, kicking and wrestling featuring largely in a protagonist s armoury. Contests staged across the States also suffered from the influence of bribery and rigging, with the lure of easy money attracting various gangsters and undesirables. One nineteenth-century ungloved bout between Irishman James Burke and Samuel O Rourke ended in a free-for-all, when

O Rourke s followers cut the ropes and stormed the ring. As Burke s entourage pitched in, firearms were produced and a riot ensued. Prior to this particular highlight, both men had enjoyed interesting careers; O Rourke was a notorious gambler and crook, while Burke once fought a 99-round marathon in which his opponent eventually died. In later years, one of the staunchest critics of the bare-knuckled art was Bob Fitzsimmons, who d seen at close quarters the damage it could cause. Although he d graduated from this particular school, with a series of ungloved scalps under his belt, he turned his back on it for good when gloved contests became the accepted form of competition. Fitzsimmons spoke of a strong distaste for bare-knuckled fighting , adding: You knock your man about so horribly, and I cannot bear the sight of a badly mauled man. This sentiment was said to have actually been shared to some extent by one of the most famous bare-knuckled artistes of the day, the infamous John L Sullivan, who became the first-ever world heavyweight champion. It was possibly the only subject the two men were ever in agreement on.

Born John Lawrence Sullivan on 15 October 1858, in Roxbury, Massachusetts, Fitzsimmons s famed counterpart and fabled godfather of prizefighting was the son of Irish immigrants. His father, who was said to have been no mean fighter himself, hailed from Tralee in County Kerry, while his mother s family originated from Athlone in County Roscommon. Sullivan was often described as a hard-drinking, hard-living bully, who was famous for knocking his opponents senseless in double-quick time. Almost single-handedly, he inspired the rise in popularity of boxing in America during the late nineteenth century, simply because of the sheer brutality of his encounters. Said to be highly volatile both in and out of the ring, it s likely he inherited his pugnacious nature from his paternal grandfather, who d been a noted Celtic wrestler. Standing at five feet ten and a half inches and weighing just under two hundred pounds, the Boston Strongboy first established his fearsome reputation in 1881, when he mercilessly battered John Flood to defeat. Flood was knocked out in all of the eight rounds, before his seconds finally threw in the sponge. Amid great secrecy, the bout was actually staged on a dusty, decrepit barge floating in the river off Hastings, near Yonkers, to avoid the attention of the police. Illustrations of the affair show both men wearing skin-tight gloves, with the Bostonian forcing his opponent onto the makeshift ropes. Flood appears to be badly cut about the face, a fact which doesn t seem to be registered in the unconcerned expressions of the well-dressed onlookers, who are watching the action with keen interest. While the audience wear frock-coats and top hats for the most part, the fighters are bare-chested, with white breeches and heavy boots. The Irishman s powerful physique is clear from the illustrations as he holds his clenched fists before him, in threatening pose. One can imagine the atmosphere, as those watching roar their charges to go in for the kill.

Perhaps inevitably, Sullivan became bare-knuckle heavyweight champion in 1882, having brutally knocked out the American champion Paddy Ryan. Such was the public clamour surrounding this fight that leading artists, dramatists and poets were sent to convey their impressions of this eagerly-awaited event, which took place in Mississipi City on 2 February. One of the most famous names among this attending number was one Oscar Wilde, who was at that time partway through an American lecture tour. A keen boxing enthusiast, he described the fight in an article for a British newspaper. What Mr Wilde thought of the proceedings is lost to time, but others reported it as an act of one-sided savagery, during which the unfortunate Ryan was virtually torn to pieces by the lethal fists of the Boston Strongboy. The rules allowed wrestling throws to be deployed during the fight and Sullivan used his size and weight advantage to hurl the American across the ring again and again. By the ninth round, Ryan was virtually unable to move and as such was immediately clubbed to the ground by the marauding Sullivan.

Sullivan bridged the worlds of bare-knuckle fighting and gloved boxing, and alternated between the two for a while, defending his bare-knuckle crown under London Prize Ring rules. By 1889, there were no more contenders for this title, and the pugnacious Irishman crossed the divide into legitimate boxing for good, remaining unbeaten in bare-knuckled bouts. Although Sullivan really belonged to the era immediately prior to that of

Fitzsimmons, the two men were once pitted against each other in a potentially explosive contest. Although the Irish-American had a few years on the Cornishman, the consequences could have been devastating. Public interest was willing it to happen, and it was due to take place in a New York hall on the night of 17 February 1897, but was unable to proceed, as the police arrived and broke up the gathering.

In later years, Sullivan was seen as the elder statesman of boxing. He would criticise Fitzsimmons for living off his fame; taking time off from title campaigns to go on tour with travelling musical shows. This can be seen as slightly ironic, as Sullivan had been accused of exactly the same thing during the later years of his own career. It was his taste for the high life and subsequent distaste for training which had actually toppled him from his throne. In any case, Fitzsimmons had little time or respect for the Bostonian, rejecting his views as those of an old has-been . Notwithstanding this opinion, Sullivan eventually turned to theatre full-time, before touring America, lecturing on the evils of alcohol.

Fitzsimmons s own bare-knuckle career had also seen its fair share of gore. One of his first professional prizefights took place in Timaru, New Zealand. He was matched against a man named Arthur Cooper, who was said to be the most promising fighter in the district at the time. It must have caused quite a stir when Cooper was soundly knocked out within three rounds by the young blacksmith, who was still combining his new-found calling with his rather more down-to-earth day job. He apparently told Cooper in the middle of a round that he was about to knock him out. Cooper laughed, and as he did, Fitzsimmons struck him to the ground with such force that the laughter immediately stopped. A later contest which was also staged without the protection of gloves was again recorded as taking place in Timaru. The opponent on this occasion was a man by the name of Jack Murphy. Fitzsimmons remembered this bout in later years, on account of its ferocity:

> Neither Murphy nor I lost any time over the preliminaries, and
> we were at it, hammer and tongs, from the off. There was a swift
> exchange in the first round, and I scored first blood with the

second punch, which landed squarely in Murphy s right eye, splitting the skin over the eyebrow. From that minute to the end of the fight, Murphy was disgusting to look at. The blood poured out in such force that anybody but as game a man as Murphy would have lain down right then. Not so he, however, for he flew at me like a wild boar with right and left, landing on my face, and as quickly again over my ribs.

Out of respect for the other man, Fitzsimmons deliberately avoided hitting him in the face over the next round, but when his own seconds urged him to finish the job he was being paid for, the hostilities warmed up once more. A punch thrown with full force from the Cornishman s mighty shoulder crashed into his opponent s mouth, splitting open both his lips. The impact of the blow drove Fitzsimmons s knuckles into Murphy s teeth, gashing the skin on his hands. Blood spurted over Fitzsimmons in such quantities that it looked as if he was bleeding as much as his counterpart. The hacking sound of Murphy coughing on his own blood could be heard throughout the next round, until a final knock-out punch put the man out of his misery. The long-term injuries suffered during such contests were often fatal, as men risked their lives for the hatful of cash which rested on the result. Some were killed, others were permanently crippled; while a few lived to fight another day, with a few more scars to show for their experience. It was after this particular bloodbath that Fitzsimmons swore never again to fight bare-knuckled.

Naturally, these feelings were shared by many. The revolution had come, back in 1866, when rules were drawn up under the sponsorship of the eighth Marquis of Queensbury, who patronised the sport back in England. These rules, which were first used in England in 1872, replaced the previous Prize Ring rules. The new regulations required boxers to wear gloves which varied between six and eight ounces in weight for professional boxers, and ten to twelve ounces for amateurs. Bouts were also divided into three-minute rounds, with a one-minute rest in between. No wrestling or gouging would be allowed, while blows would have to be struck fairly and squarely with the gloved fists. Each man would have to keep his gloves raised, in order to best defend himself. Blows below the belt would be illegal, along with those to the back of the head. Should a fighter be knocked to the ground, he would be given ten seconds — the doleful decimal — in which to regain himself. A count by the referee would mark this time, and should the boxer be unable to get up before the count was completed, a knockout would be declared. These rules have, by and large, stayed in place until the current day; and while many claim that boxing is still a barbaric sport, they can at least reflect that it s far less barbaric than it was at the outset of Fitzsimmons s fighting days.

To pursue his dream of becoming a professional prizefighter, the young Robert Fitzsimmons took a drastic personal step when he decided to leave the confines of his adopted country for the more promising opportunities on offer in Australia. In doing so, he echoed the sentiments of his parents some years before, when they departed from Helston to put down roots in a foreign country, where opportunities beckoned more readily.

If the decision to move to Sydney was prompted by his boxing ambitions, Fitzsimmons s personal life seems to have adjusted remarkably well to the change in lifestyle. He made the trip with Alice, his childhood sweetheart, although there are conflicting reports as to whether the two were married prior to making the move, or if they officially tied the knot on arriving in Sydney. In any case, their eventual marriage was blessed with a child, a boy whom they christened Charles. And although Bob was juggling his ring appearances with his day job, he would actually prosper in the latter as well, eventually setting up his own forge. But just as all seemed to be rosy, an incident occurred which would see the Cornishman make all the wrong sort of headlines.

On the night of 10 February 1890, in the city of Sydney, Bob was billed to fight a man named Jem Hall. Hall had already made something of a name for himself — a middleweight who was being counted among the country s brightest sporting hopes. The Sydney native, a former plasterer, held the Australian middleweight championship, having beaten Peter Boland in Victoria on 11 January 1890. Standing six feet and one inch tall, and weighing in at around eleven stone four pounds, he was bigger and stronger than Fitzsimmons, besides being his junior by four years. Against his current run of impressive form, the evening would see young Fitzsimmons suffer his first ever defeat, as he was decisively knocked down and counted out during the fourth round. It came as something of a surprise to the growing number of fans and commentators who d been following the young fighter s career, and marked a significant blip on his chart of progress. Almost at once, Fitzsimmons was being accused of over-reaching, of having ideas well above his station. Critics were quick to hold this fight up as evidence that the Cornishman was not worthy of championship speculation; that he was simply outclassed when up against quality opposition. These claims would ring in his ears for years to come, as his career path suddenly reached a crossroads. It was at this junction that his future as a fighter would be decided — whether he would join the great and the good, or merely descend into the faceless crowds of also-rans who populated the sport s lower reaches. Subsequent revelations would throw further light on the episode revealing that — once again — all was not as it seemed, and that an element of gamesmanship had crept into the ring that night. Hall, unsurprisingly, was quick to take credit for a notable victory, crowing that he d been the better man on the day, which — he was quick to point out — was all that mattered. He and his camp would later cast aspersions on Fitzsimmons s title hopes, denigrating him as a one-hit wonder; a small-time fighter who would soon be relegated to the fairground sideshow. When interviewed about the subject almost twenty years later — such was the controversy which still dogged the issue — Hall was still denying that he d engaged Bob s theatrical skills, rather than his fighting talents. He explained: Fitz and I were matched for five hundred dollars a-side and the gate receipts. There is nothing in the Sydney Referee to show there was any laying-down on Bob s part. It was a square stand-up fight and the blow that finished Fitz was as fast a one as ever I landed. He uncovered his jaw for a moment and I sent one over that dropped him at my feet and he was out , well and truly. I had to skip lively to get out of his way as he fell. Fitzsimmons s own verdict on the story was, equally predictably, somewhat different. While accepting that he d lost the fight, he would later explain his reasons for doing so, blaming the corruption which still plagued the sport for his adverse result. He said of the Hall fight:

> Had I known half as much of the crookedness of the roped arena as any amateur knows now, the result would have been very different . . . the decision was given to Hall, and the reason for it is the one blot on my career. It was done quite unintentionally on my part, and without any knowledge of the consequences or the appearance of it. I knew nothing of betting at the time, and was not aware that a single penny was wagered on the result believing that the small purse we were each to receive was all there was to it.

He claimed he could have beaten Hall easily from the moment the fight started, being his superior in every way. I could have ended his fistic aspirations with one wallop, he boasted, once more displaying his unique blend of diplomacy and modesty. Fitzsimmons alleged that the fight had been deliberately rigged, and that he had been duped into playing along with it, by one of his own backers. This man, whose name he never revealed, had apparently claimed that unless the decision went Hall s way, he wouldn t get any money from the event. Pleading with the young boxer, he begged him to throw the fight. Always a soft touch, Fitzsimmons seemed to swallow the story without question. Tearfully, he told me of his wife and seven children at home, and said no harm could come of it, if I allowed Hall to give me the worst of it, but unless I lost, he would lose his home. A rather more worldly-wise man would almost certainly have thrown the dubious plea back in the promoter s face, but in this case, a mixture of naivety and good nature won the day. It was almost certainly this lack of worldliness which led the promoter to make the approach in the first place. Subsequently, Fitzsimmons admitted that he did indeed take a dive . Rather than see my good friend suffer so much loss, I allowed a swing to land, instead of parrying it, and down I went to my first defeat. Respect — albeit misguided — for his colleague had left Fitzsimmons with little or no choice, as he saw it.

After the fight, it s claimed that Fitzsimmons never received the bribe he was promised for falling down, and it s likely this is what really irked him at the time; that Hall should get the glory, and not keep his side of the bargain. Fitzsimmons was fuming at this turn of events, and vented his anger by hammering furiously at horseshoes in the forge over the next few days, presumably wishing it was Hall s head he was re-shaping.

Fitz was keen to reverse the decision immediately in a re-match, but — strangely enough — Hall was less than enthusiastic. I was promised another go to prove my superiority, but the occasion never came. I followed him about, and offered to fight for nothing, with Hall to take all that would be paid for the two of us, but he would never meet me, he complained.

As well as a short-term financial deficit with a young family to support, there was a bigger price to pay, one which Bob may not have fully realised at the time. Audiences don t pay to see play-acting, they pay to see fights. And the loss, coupled with the mysterious circumstances surrounding it, would cast a shadow of suspicion over him for some time to come. Ironically, the paths of the two fighters were about to cross again soon, as both men — although they didn t know it yet — were about to launch professional careers in America. Fitzsimmons once actually went so far as to claim that the only reason he emigrated to America was that it would give him the opportunity of fighting Hall again. He told a story of the two arriving at the docks simultaneously, with Fitzsimmons catching an earlier boat, and Hall watching him off, as the sea opened up the miles between them.

Almost certainly, this is Fitzsimmons s over-active imagination at work. For the two fighters to be departing on the same day would be an outrageous co-incidence, and in any case, to uproot yourself and your family to start a new life in another country all on the premise of righting a wrong with one man would have been foolhardy, even for him. The two did depart for foreign shores within a short space of time, but, as we ll see later, each had his own agenda for doing so.

Meanwhile, the promising Australian was being groomed as a possible championship contender, with a chance of being lined up to meet the great Jack Dempsey in America. This was perhaps the real reason for the fight with Fitzsimmons, and could go some way to explaining the skullduggery which surrounded it. The thinking of Hall s backers was that a victory over a live-wire like Fitzsimmons would give Hall a significant scalp under his belt before he travelled to San Francisco. For an aspiring middle-weight, the opportunity to meet such a legend in the ring was confirmation that you d really scaled the dizzy heights of your sport. Ironically, it was Dempsey who d actually play a significant part in Fitzsimmons s career in the coming years. For the moment, however, it was Hall who was to be packaged and sold as the great new hope, and the defeat of Fitzsimmons would have reached ears on the other side of the water; people would not realise what a complete fiasco it had been.

It was while rowdily celebrating this victory that Hall proved that some fighters really do keep their brains in their fists. With a world championship career only days away, he got involved in a drunken bar brawl, and suffered stab wounds in the ensuing fight. His hand was wounded so seriously that the forthcoming American trip was immediately deemed to be out of the question. With Hall out of the picture for the time being, another name was put up — that of Fitzsimmons. Many believed he had actually given the better account of himself in the recent bout, even if they didn t know the reason for the result. Tom James, a ship s purser sent to Australia to escort Hall to the California Athletic Club, made the same offer to Bob. Fitzsimmons s reply was that he would have to ask the missus . It seems this all-important permission was forthcoming. Alice would almost certainly have been attracted by the possibilities which abounded in the States. She had ambitions at the time to pursue her own theatrical career, so this would have seemed to be a good move all round. As they weren t able to leave straight away, because of Bob s commitments at the blacksmith s, an arrangement was struck, the Fitzsimmons family making their way to California under their own steam.

This heaven-sent opportunity to brave a shot at a major title had dropped in the Cornishman s lap because of Hall, much to the chagrin of the latter. Because of this, there was always an animosity between the two men. Fitzsimmons was still sore at being duped into throwing the fight. Hall was sore at Fitzsimmons for taking his place in America. Years later, the story would have a happy ending as far as the Cornishman was concerned — the re-match with Hall did actually come about. It was originally due to be staged on 22 July 1891 in Minneapolis; but the authorities got wind of the arrangements and managed to prevent it. Only until two years later, when the pair met once more, this time in New Orleans on 8 March 1893. The bout was contesting the world middleweight championship; and if Fitzsimmons was still holding a grudge, he well and truly exorcised it that night, flattening Hall in an efficient display of fistic skill. The one-sided contest served as further evidence that their original meeting had, indeed, been fixed.

According to boxing historian Gilbert Odd, the voyage from Australia didn t pass entirely without incident. Before Fitzsimmons had even set foot on American soil, he was already making waves, it seemed. Bored and restless throughout the twenty-four-day epic journey, he was doing two of the things he did best: causing mischief and upsetting people. As a game, he would wait for a burly purser or crew member to walk by on deck, and deliberately trip him up; causing the unfortunate victim to fall in a heap. When they angrily remonstrated with him, he would goad them further, until a fight ensued. As his opponents tried to strike him, Bob would use his best defensive skills to deftly dodge and deflect each punch, prancing round the aggressor, without ever trying to land a blow himself. To the amusement of those nearby, and to the frustration of the furious sailors, this would continue until the attacker eventually tired. All who witnessed this horseplay would marvel at Fitzsimmons s uncanny speed and agility. Mr Odd reports that the Cornishman s super-fast reflexes caught the eye of one John Brewer, an American pigeon shot champion, who was returning from a competition in Melbourne. Brewer later told a newspaper journalist about Fitzsimmons: He is a fearless man who does not know what the word danger means. Referring to the play-fights, he said that Fitzsimmons was like a big kid . The same journalist, Ed Cole, was advised by his own betting brother in Australia to bet five hundred quid on the blacksmith for me, no matter who he fights, and don t forget to put down a good bet for yourself. He is a phenomenal man.

Fitzsimmons was met by a representative of the California Athletic Club, who had invited him in the first place. Carrying a letter of introduction from AG Hales, a sportswriter who d refereed the fight with Hall, Fitzsimmons was temporarily accommodated at the home of Barney Farley, a local sportsman. Early publicity photographs showing the Cornishman adorned in top hat and dress suit are due in part to Farley, as the young blacksmith had borrowed that man s clothes in order to look gentlemanly . Whether or not he achieved this rather grand aim, Fitzsimmons was clearly attempting to take his place in American society.

On the day he arrived in San Francisco, Bob was granted an audience with Lam Fulda, who held the position of President at the California Athletic Club. As they d originally been expecting Jim Hall, Fitz was something of an unknown quantity, despite the recommendations they d received from Australia. It was decided that a test bout should be arranged, in which they would be able to gauge his potential. The new immigrant was characteristically nonchalant about this test, remarking that he d fight anyone, whenever they liked. His less-than-imposing appearance hadn t filled his new sponsors with a great deal of confidence, so they may have been forgiven for harbouring some doubts as to his real potential. A fight was hastily arranged with a promising local middleweight who went by the name of Frank Allen. This took place just a few days after Bob s arrival, on the evening of 17 May 1890. Among those in attendance were a gathering of club representatives, all of whom were curious as to what they d let themselves in for in bringing this rather odd-looking chap to America. It s not much of an overstatement to say that the events which unfolded during the course of that evening would dramatically change the course of Fitzsimmons s career, and even alter the course of boxing history in America.

From the outset, Allen was simply blown away; hit from one side of the ring to another, buckling under a relentless barrage of blows from the highly charged newcomer. The home-grown talent was clearly way out of his league; trying and failing to land a punch on

PRIZE FIGHTER

Fitz, before being battered to the floor again. The speed and efficiency of the Cornishman s movements and the sheer power with which he slammed punches into Allen s flailing head meant that the fight was reduced to a one-sided showcase. It wasn t long before the ritual slaughter was brought to an abrupt end, as a shattering right-hand blow knocked Allen out cold. After the fight, it was discovered that he had broken a wrist, and had had part of his valuable dentistry smashed to pieces under the onslaught. Clearly, the members of the California Athletic Club were going to have to be more choosy about whom they let in the ring with this man Fitzsimmons, if they didn t want their best fighters getting seriously hurt.

After some searching, a man was found who was thought to be potentially capable of stopping Fitz in his tracks. He was Billy McCarthy, another migr from Australia, who d held the middleweight title while in that country. He d actually sparred with Fitzsimmons some years previously, when the young blacksmith was first finding his feet, and so he felt confident of his chances. He said at the time: They offered a purse of 1,250 dollars for me to meet Fitzsimmons in a substitute match, and having sparred four rounds at the Iron Pot [a boxing club] in Sydney, where I was instructing for Larry Foley, I readily agreed to meet him again as I did not think he would be hard to beat. They say pride comes before a fall, and never are those words more significant than in boxing, where to drop one s guard — either physically or mentally — will see you take a painful fall before very long. McCarthy was certainly guilty of failing to take the forthcoming fight seriously, as he had recently taken the world champion Jack Dempsey to twenty-eight rounds, and had valiantly fought numerous men with far more experience than his latest opponent. An important factor, also, is the change which Fitzsimmons had undergone since their first meeting; from an awkward, inexperienced part-timer, to a hungry, dedicated professional. While he didn t have the numerous ring-hours of local pros, nor the awesome reputation of the great Dempsey, he possessed guts and ability in abundance, as McCarthy was about to find out.

The two men pulled on the gloves on the evening of 29 May

1890. As they both stepped into the ring, a hail of laughter is said to have greeted the Cornishman, as the boxing public inspected him properly for the first time. When he slipped out of his dressing gown, his skinny legs drew hoots of derision, with all bets placed firmly in McCarthy s corner. Most men present would have bet their next paycheque on the former middleweight champion putting this cocky newcomer firmly in his place. They would have regretted doing so. When the two men came together in the ring, Fitzsimmons unleashed a huge punch which connected flush in McCarthy s face, knocking him clean off his feet. You could have heard a pin drop in the hall, as the favourite crashed down onto the canvas and lay there half-stunned. The bout was less than a minute old, and a respected middleweight veteran had been pole-axed with virtually the first punch of the fight. Eyebrows were raised, and headlines hastily composed. America was about to sit up and take notice of this wild young man, who was said to fight as if he had the very devil in him. Having groggily picked himself up, the humiliated McCarthy was relentlessly pursued around the ring for the rest of the first round, breathlessly running away from the determined Cornishman. Having only just survived until the bell, he was punched senseless over the next few rounds, sinking to the canvas several times, without offering any kind of effective resistance. His composure in tatters, he was clearly re-thinking his views on the man who was destroying him so comprehensively.

He should have thrown in the towel immediately, and in modern times no right-thinking referee would have let such a bloodbath continue. But pride forced him to endure this most terrible punishment, until he resorted to foul tactics in the sixth round. Having just received another numbing combination of blows to the head, he threw a crafty punch which caught Fitzsimmons way below the belt, causing him to crumple up in pain. This was an ill-advised move for two reasons; one, it was by now illegal, and almost caused the referee to stop the fight and disqualify him. Two, it infuriated his opponent, and made him even more determined than he had been previously. To the crowd s appreciation, and McCarthy s consternation, Fitz insisted that the fight should continue. He obviously wanted the victory to be as emphatic as it was deserved. He was granted his wish towards the end of the ninth round, when McCarthy finally could take no more, and slid to the ground and was counted out. It had been a great victory for the Cornishman, and a great show for the crowd. Many people leaving the hall that night would have been discussing the former blacksmith s world-class potential. Before very long it was a topic which would be discussed across the length and breadth of the United States.

The winning purse from the McCarthy fight would have convinced Fitzsimmons that this truly was the land of opportunity, as it was likely to have amounted to more than the sum total of all his previous bouts. What s more, his ruthless demolition of his opponent was helping to garner a reputation as the Australian Wonder , especially as it had taken the fearsome Jack Dempsey three times as long to knock out the same man, only three months before. One of the important factors in his performance had been his seemingly inexhaustible stamina. This he had achieved with the help of some gruelling training runs along the Californian coast, much to the despair of his training partners, who were left gasping by his enthusiastic canters. One of them, a featherweight named Freddy Brogan, remarked that no-one could keep up with the crazy Cornishman nor last anywhere near as long.

Bob s next fight was intended to send out a message to the American public; one that ensured his successes so far wouldn t be written off as beginner s luck. It was hoped by his backers that the reigning champions of the time would also hear this message, and be prepared to risk their reputations and their titles. It seems incredible that an unknown fighter who d been in the country a matter of weeks would be considered for future title-bouts, but those who d seen him in action couldn t imagine him being beaten, such was his presence in the ring.

His next opponent was a man named Arthur Upham, who hailed from Nova Scotia. Wearing five-ounce gloves, the men would compete for a purse of one thousand dollars, with the winner receiving 60 per cent, and the loser 40 per cent. The fight was arranged to take place on 28 June 1890 at the Audubon Athletic Club in New Orleans. If any doubts remained about Fitzsimmons being the hottest prizefighting prospect in America, they were surely dispelled that night. Upham was a respected boxer who outweighed Fitzsimmons by around half-a-stone. Regardless of this, in the fifth round, he was hit so hard that he was unconscious before he landed on the canvas. The sight of the outstretched man, lying out cold on the floor of the ring, would have sent a chilling message to all those who would take on the Cornishman in the future. It wasn t long before the buzz being created on the West Coast reached the ears of one Jack Dempsey, at his luxurious home in Portland, Oregon. Promoters were keen to stage this fight of the year, which would see the unbeaten superstar challenged by the hungry young pretender to his throne. In his ten-year career, Dempsey had defended his title five times, gaining a god-like status as America s national prizefighting hero. Dismissing Fitzsimmons as a no-hoper, he accepted the challenge, and agreed to meet the man from Cornwall in a contest for the middleweight champion-ship of the world. It would take place at a venue in the state of Louisiana. This was the fight everyone was waiting to see.

4. The King is Dead ... Long Live the King

New Orleans, USA
14 January 1891

To the outsider, there seemed no contest. Jack Dempsey — the tough, battle-hardened brawler who rejoiced in the name Nonpareil — man without equal. Opposing him, a raw, unblooded Cornish immigrant, seemingly drawn to the prize money and the bright flame of overnight fame. Most people considered he was destined to suffer much the same fate as the unfortunate moth which flies too close to that flame. This was due to the fact that Dempsey s fame and reputation had reached the far corners of the world. People took a macabre interest in his annihilation of opponents, carried out in the same. clinical manner that a pathologist dissects a cadaver. With fists like steam-hammers, Dempsey battered opponents like a man swatting flies from his path. Feared and respected in equal amounts on both sides of the ropes he was *the* fighter to beat at the time. Every contest sent a current of excitement through the sporting world, quickly followed by a wave of sympathy for the intended victim . On the other hand, the man challenging him was unknown and without any substantial reputation or track record. As if this wasn t bad enough, he was an Englishman imported from Australia. The odds on Fitzsimmons beating Dempsey when they went man to man were thought to be somewhere between the remote and the impossible. If appearances were anything to go by those doubters may indeed have had a point. The twenty-seven-year-old Cornish expatriate was muscular and lean around the chest and shoulders, but his legs were almost comically thin, and his general build looked completely at odds to that of the husky brawlers of the day. From a modern-day perspective, it can be compared to an unknown fighter from

Britain s backstreet training gyms taking on Mike Tyson at Caesar s Palace in Las Vegas. Bold and impertinent, Fitzsimmons was seen as a figure of ridicule; a cocky young upstart who d be taught a much-needed lesson when he finally came face to face with the fearsome Dempsey. His recent victories since arriving on American shores counted for nothing in this hallowed company.

At the time of meeting Fitzsimmons, he held the world middleweight title — a division which had first been established in England in 1786, when Gentleman Richard Humphries defeated the Jewish fighter Daniel Mendoza. The class traditionally consisted of men weighing in at around eleven stone. In the early days, for a contest to be considered a world championship, the fighters had to be champion of the Old World — England — and the New World —America. The first of these contests took place in April 1860, between the Englishman Tom Sayers and the American John C Heenan. But it was when the likes of Dempsey arrived on the scene, with his razor-sharp reflexes and inordinate skill with his fists, that fighters began to be recognised as household names. The burly brawler had gained an awesome reputation, flooring such opponents as Jack Fogerty, George LaBlanche and Johny Reagan. The contest with Reagan had been an epic battle, lasting no fewer than forty-five rounds. Born John Kelly in 1852, back in Kilrain, Ireland, Dempsey s roots, like many fighters of the time, lay in the unlicensed bare-knuckle scraps rather than the regulated sport which was beginning to take over. A number of his early fights had been raided by police.

Having established his place among the early sporting celebrities, Dempsey was clearly keen to avoid relinquishing it. It can therefore be assumed that when he agreed to take on the new boy in town , he didn t consider him too much of a threat. Not that he had any reason to — at that time, the challenger was almost literally just off the boat. Little was generally known about his record, other than the fact that he d enjoyed some success in the bare-knuckle rings of the Antipodes. Fitzsimmons was potentially just another member of an ever-growing band of hopefuls, has-beens, never-will-bes and journeymen, managing to earn a half-decent living from their hazardous profession before descending into the twilight world of bouncers, fairground fighters and strong-arm men. So it was against this background that dismissive attitudes towards Fitzsimmons were formed.

Typically, Fitzsimmons s preparations for the biggest fight of his life didn t pass entirely without incident. It was a sign of things to come. The trouble started when he fell out with his manager and trainer English Jimmy . James Carroll was himself a former bare-knuckle fighter, originally hailing from Lambeth in South London. He d fought numerous times in America as a lightweight before taking Fitz under his wing. A row at the training camp led to Carroll storming off, apparently for good. He was to seek solace in the bottom of a bottle, an unwise course of action that worsened an already tense situation. Fitzsimmons — always quick to take umbrage — was furious, and threatened to cut his manager out of their usual business arrangement. I was so sore at Carroll for leaving me in the lurch at the last minute that I told one of his closest friends that I would cut him out of the deal unless he returned that day, Fitzsimmons later said. His wife came to see me at once, and assured me that he would be back at noon. I promised that if he was, I would overlook his desertion. Unfortunately, when Carroll did return to the gym where Bob was enthusiastically walloping a punchbag, the errant manager was said to be very much the worse for drink. Inevitably, the volatile fighter had plenty to say on this and other related subjects, and another colourful row ensued, which ended in Carroll stamping off once more, with the parting shot: Dempsey will punch your head off tomorrow night.

It may have been true that Fitzsimmons was capable of starting an argument in an empty house but on this occasion he considered himself justified in withholding Carroll s share of the prospective spoils. It was only a last-minute change of heart on his behalf that saved the situation, when he realised he couldn t face a champion of Dempsey s stature without a very astute tactician in his corner. Carroll had had previous experience with Dempsey and it was considered vital that this expertise be made available to the Cornish challenger. The two were a team once more, but nerves would have been jangling even more loudly than usual, as last-minute preparations drew to a close.

THE KING IS DEAD ... LONG LIVE THE KING

Even by the somewhat loose standards of nineteenth-century prize-ring venues, the old Olympic Club in New Orleans was somewhat lacking in terms of facilities. A gentleman s club it wasn t — the ring itself was simply a square of earth, tastefully surrounded by a six-foot-high barbed-wire fence. Anyone attending the fight would have no doubts about the serious nature of the event; but in case any of the rougher element in the audience was tempted to scale the fence and try to influence the proceedings within, the captain of the local police force had stated that if anyone so much as put a hand on it, he would shoot him where he stood . Security aside, the irrepressible Fitzsimmons had somehow managed to upset the same police chief during the pre-fight warm-up, as he negotiated a side-bet with Dempsey while they stood in their ring costumes. Dempsey offered a thousand-pound wager on the winner, and promoter Major Frank McGlaucklin offered to stump up Bob s stake. The police captain hastily stepped in at this point, and stated there was to be no betting inside the ring. It was time to fight.

The crowd roared, bayed and booed in a high-pitched frenzy of noise. All were on their feet, craning for a better view, with their shouts and cries raining down on the two bare-chested men in the centre of the dirt ring. The reason for the furore — Jack Dempsey, the decorated veteran of the fight game, was gingerly picking himself up from the dust, having been cut down in his prime; ignominiously despatched to the ground by the blistering speed of the challenger. Dempsey s legions of fans were staring in open-mouthed disbelief at their hero, as he scrambled awkwardly to his feet. The shock was also apparent in the opposing corner: they couldn t believe what their man had actually done. It was Fitzsimmons s finest hour to date. He was out-boxing, out-manoeuvring and outsmarting the hapless champion. The punch which had first sent Dempsey sprawling would have stopped any fighter anywhere, such was its venomous force. With one blow, the former blacksmith had elevated himself from the anonymous rank and file, to become one of the new celebrities of the ring. Having already lost his dignity, Jack Dempsey was now also in imminent danger of losing his title, as the punch which had felled him drained most of his strength. He was also in shock at such an unexpected role-reversal. Teetering on wobbling legs, he launched a half-hearted riposte against Fitzsimmons, but his attack was smoothly parried, before a sweeping left hook connected with a numbing force, dropping him to the floor once more in a dusty cloud. It was a position which would have been previously unthinkable. Bob Fitzsimmons had a cool, clinical sense of purpose and the calm precision of a seasoned professional. Like a rat in a trap, Dempsey looked for a way of stopping the punishment. There was none.

It wasn t just the feat Fitzsimmons had achieved — it was the calculated way in which it had been executed. The power which Fitzsimmons expelled from his taut, muscled frame had been too much for Dempsey, whose head had been repeatedly whipped back onto his shoulders with an onslaught of blow after blow. Under fire, his legs buckling, he d hastily retreated from the advancing Cornishman. But it was too late. Too, too late. In a few short moments, the balance of power between these two had been won and lost. For round after round, the slaughter continued. Despite his desperate efforts, the champion was unable to land a punch on the sprightly challenger. Bloodsport fans would have cheered as Dempsey displayed the stubborn willpower which had once taken him to the top of his industry. But it was an exercise in damage limitation. Frantically clinging onto the dying hopes of a fast-evaporating salvation, the veteran held, parried and blocked as best he could, all the while trying to avoid the viper-strike of Fitzsimmons s deadly fists. There was only ever going to be one possible outcome. At one point, Fitzsimmons even relented, holding his fire to offer his bloodied colleague an honourable exit: retire from the carnage and admit defeat. It was a gesture of respect, a tribute to the beaten man s standing and reputation. But Dempsey shook his head, refusing the gentlemanly option. He stood defiant before his opponent, daring him to finish the job off. Bleeding heavily, his face was swollen and disfigured by the beating it had suffered, but his spirit refused to suffer the same fate. It was perhaps the last remnants of his pride which kept him going, which continued to spur him on in the face of such fearsome punishment.

Finally, he could take no more. In the thirteenth round he slumped into the mud. The giant had been slain. It had been a bloody battle which would be remembered for many years to come.

Finally, Nonpareil had met his equal.

Ironically, the beating proved to be the foundation of a firm but short-lived friendship between Fitzsimmons and Dempsey. Dempsey only made only three more ring appearances. He died four years later. On his death-bed Dempsey advised his wife to bet all her money on Fitzsimmons, no matter who he was fighting. Only during an era when men were required to do such serious physical damage to each other in the name of competition, can such a relationship be fully understood. Those who lived through it understood without question. There was a mutual respect between men who were brave enough to pit their bodies against each other in such a dramatic fashion.

Years later, Fitzsimmons recalled the Dempsey fight as one of the most memorable and exciting of my career , describing his opponent as being just the gamest man that ever put up his hands to defend himself . He recounted: The papers were saying that it was simply butchery. I had punished him unmercifully, and I myself wondered however a man could take such punishment . . . The result lost me many friends, for everybody loved Jack Dempsey. But others had noticed the gentlemanly gesture which had been made by the eventual victor. One of America s leading sports writers, Robert Edgren, said in the *New York Evening World* of the new champion:

> With all his gameness and marvellous fighting skill, and with all his wonderful knock-out powers, Fitzsimmons was always the fairest and most generous of fighters. When he fought the great Nonpareil for the middleweight championship, Fitz beat Dempsey down time and again . . . Whispering, Fitzsimmons begged Dempsey to stay down. Generous even in the greatest victory of his early fighting career, he didn t want to injure the

defeated man by cutting him up even more, or by finishing him
with one of his terrible knock-out blows.

Sentiment aside, Dempsey had been soundly beaten, and Bob
Fitzsimmons, of Helston, Cornwall, was now the middleweight
champion of the world.

5. Without Equal

The bloody battle of New Orleans would forever transform the lives of both Dempsey and Fitzsimmons, marking an irreversible turning-point in both of their careers. It was from this staging post that the world of championship prizefighting had passed into a new incarnation. The unbeatable champion had, at last, been indisputably beaten. His air of invincibility had been run through with Fitzsimmons s sharp blade, and it seemed certain his formidable reputation would never carry quite the same foreboding again. His was an honourable defeat, however, with his dignified courage in the face of a better man shining brightly throughout the emphatic victory. While he wore his mask of dignity in the ring, however, it was apparently a different story as soon as he was carried from it, as he wept all the way back to the dressing room. Almost certainly, he was weeping as much for his injured pride as for his lost title. Contorted by the pain of his injuries he s said to have groaned to his seconds: It would not hurt nearly so much had I been beaten by an Irishman or an American. But to have it handed to me by a ****ing Englishman has killed me!

While Fitzsimmons would certainly have welcomed this colourful tribute, he would probably claim that he wasn t an Englishman, he was a Cornishman. But the fact remained that he had been catapulted from the position of an unknown rank outsider to that of an excitingly hot property. It seemed as if the entire fight world was talking of his seemingly limitless prospects. Those present on the fateful night told those rather less fortunate souls how the young immigrant had moved quickly and deftly about the ring, hitting Dempsey from all angles with a force and accuracy the like of which had never been seen before in an American ring. He had wordlessly ridiculed those harsh critics who d written him off as a lanky freak . He d proved that his slight build masked a crafty cunning and a lethal finishing power, which could be unleashed in a one-on-one fight. From now on, he would be a man to watch, as he hungrily took on all comers in search of fame, stardom and glory — his ultimate goals.

He was quick to defend his newly-won title, completely annihilating the highly-rated New Zealander Dan Creedon, in a ridiculously one-sided contest. At that time, it seemed as if the Cornish boxer with the lightning fists was virtually invincible, as one opponent after another was outshone by his sleight of hand, and punished swiftly and summarily by his deadly reflexes. Creedon himself later proved he was no pushover, by going on to win the English middleweight and heavyweight titles. But it was Fitzsimmons who was capturing all the news headlines, as America focused its attention on this boxer. Fighters from around the world were hastily lined up to meet him, as he risked his title time and again, taking on men far bigger and stronger than himself. Each was keen to chance his arm against this deceptively frail-looking champion. But in this quest, all would fall miserably short of the mark. One after another, promising hopefuls with impeccable records were punched out of contention — their forlorn title hopes crashing to the ground with them. All were humiliatingly wrong-footed by a natural talent which was both raw and explosive, in the way it preyed on opponents weaknesses and mistakes with the pace of a rattlesnake. When the sweeping, bony left fist connected with its victim s head and body, there would only ever be one possible outcome. Poker-faced and stony-handed, the muscular blacksmith cut down the cream of the current crop of fighters, as he entered the prime of his career — the glory years.

During the remaining part of 1891, he soundly demolished Abe Cougle of Chicago within two rounds, and did the same to the exotically-named Black Pearl, who lasted four rounds. These two meetings were part of a travelling show, in which the new champion would bet local fighters that they couldn t spar a few rounds with him. Anyone with any sense who d witnessed his chilling demolition of the great Jack Dempsey would almost certainly have gone out of their way to avoid stepping into the ring.

With the advent of 1892, Fitzsimmons stopped Peter Maher in twelve rounds in New Orleans, before subsequently going on to knock out James Farrell in two rounds, Joe Godfrey in one, and Jerry Slattery in two. The bout with Maher was a long and bloody one in which the giant Irishman tested the champion far beyond the bounds of his previous fights. But Fitz was found to possess guts as well as strength, and fought until Maher could no longer withstand the prolonged and agonising punishment. Blood poured from the Irishman s mouth, which had been badly torn by Fitzsimmons s knuckles. Both battered and bloodied, the two men reportedly shared a conciliatory bottle of whisky after the fight — true to form, the share of spoils was again somewhat uneven: Maher took one gulp; Bob drained the rest. The Slattery encounter was also a colourful one — the challenger was one of several tough dockers from New York s Bowery district who climbed into the touring ring to chance his arm. After sparring for a while, he seized his chance when Fitz dropped his guard, landing a wild punch, flush on the champ s chin. Slattery would have been well advised to leave the ring there and then, as the lucky blow induced a rare temper in Fitz, which saw the heavily-built Irishman rendered unconscious a few minutes later.

The next contender, Millard Zeuder, lasted only one punch before he sank to the floor, and slid back into anonymity. The variety circuit around America was littered with prostrate boxers, who d been foolish enough to think they could defeat the new sensation. A characteristic of all of these fights was Fitzsimmons s total and absolute control over the proceedings. He toyed with them, he let them stay in the ring, he danced around them. But when his chosen moment to end the fight came, the fight ended. There and then. And there was apparently nothing anyone could do about it, regardless of skill, size or experience. His natural exuberance and penchant for exaggeration aside, there was little doubt that he held the future of prizefighting in his muscular hands at this point in history. The carnage continued throughout the following year, with victims falling at the Cornishman s feet including Phil Mayo, Baltimore Warner and Jack Hickey. After several months of this, there was a lull in the supply of volunteers, as the likelihood of lasting more than a few rounds seemed increasingly remote.

Fitzsimmons laughed off derogatory comments about his lack of stature, deriding those who thought brawn was the answer in overcoming his talents. He boasted of being ready to accept any challenge, from anyone, anywhere in the world. The bigger they are, the harder they fall, was the immortal phrase he coined; a phrase which has passed into general usage by all of those who choose to fight when the odds are stacked against them. By this time, Bob was accustomed to receiving the adulation which was poured upon his muscular shoulders. F ted as a celebrity wherever he went, it was a side of life which he had never even heard of, let alone experienced. But he took to it naturally; as though it was his by divine right. For him, it was something to savour and enjoy, rather than resent; an integral part of the dream he d craved for so long.

Around the time of Bob s clash with the unfortunate Millard Zeuder, a contest was being staged in New Orleans, which — although he didn t know it at the time — would have a significent effect on Fitzsimmons s future. Far away in a three-day festival of boxing, there was a star attraction among all the bouts taking place. To contest the heavyweight championship of the world, the great champion John L Sullivan would take on the challenger from San Francisco, James Gentleman Jim Corbett. Although it s likely that the two heavyweights had heard of the man who d been grabbing the headlines in the middleweight division, neither of them knew that Bob Fitzsimmons had travelled to New Orleans, having just fought in Anneston, Alabama. Fitzsimmons was subsequently among the crowd which saw Corbett take the title from Sullivan, partly due to the former s devotion to the gym, and the latter s devotion to good living. In any case, Fitz refused to be cowed by such illustrious company, and told all who d listen after the contest that he was less than impressed with their showing. He told reporters that he, a mere middleweight, could take on Corbett and beat him. After all, he explained, Peter Maher was a heavyweight, and look what had happened to him . . .

When he later heard about Fitzsimmons s proclamations, Corbett was deeply insulted that a fighter significantly smaller than himself should have had the impudence to challenge him so boldly. So he sent word back that Fitzsimmons would be well advised to keep his comments to himself. This sound advice was neither wanted nor heeded. Instead, it proved to be the opening parry in a feud which would carry on for many years to come; and in comparison to their later exchanges, it was positively cordial. Meanwhile, another person who d had his feathers ruffled by the controversial newcomer was now in town with an urgent score to settle. Jem Hall, still smarting from the disastrous Australian bar-room brawl, had arrived in San Francisco. He was most put out to hear that the man who d replaced him on the trip to the States had taken the country by storm, and that he was well on his way to becoming one of its best-known sporting celebrities. Having attended the Maher fight in New Orleans, Hall dramatically climbed into the ring, to issue a challenge to the Cornishman who d taken what he saw as his rightful place in America. Hall felt he d been hard done by since the pair last met; after all, he d officially beaten Bob on that occasion! Promoters love nothing better than a grudge. So a bout was eventually arranged to take place in New Orleans, after much to-ing and fro-ing over contracts and conditions.

The two were due to meet on 8 March 1893; although the fight was close to being called off when the host club s officials refused to hand over more than one thousand dollars of the ticket money. Fitzsimmons s manager tried to persuade Bob to withdraw, but the Cornishman declined, fearing it would affect his reputation. The moment of truth arrived at around 9 p.m. when Fitzsimmons and Hall touched gloves for the first time since their ill-fated clash back in Australia. While putting on an impressive display of ringplay, neither was giving much ground until the third round, when Hall seemed to be pressing Fitzsimmons for a result. That result came in the very next round. But it was the opposite of that which Hall had intended. A dropped guard on his behalf led to a lightning-fast right-hand punch from Fitz, which connected full in the Australian s face, dumping him onto the canvas. He lay motionless.

The fight was over, and a more emphatic result could hardly be imagined. The bad blood between the two men had been purged, with only a small amount actually being spilt in that New Orleans arena.

There was a sting in the tail for Fitzsimmons, however. While celebrating the fact that he remained world champion, he discovered that his purse from the fight was far less than he d imagined. Only five thousand dollars to be exact, and although he successfully sued the promoters for a further thirteen thousand, a proportion of this was eaten up by the subsequent legal fees. For a bout which had attracted around eight thousand spectators, this was short of the mark — a situation which had arisen from Fitz s own rash decision to fight. Not for the first time, the Cornishman s success in the ring failed to be duplicated at the bank.

There was another reason for the cock-up over the financial affairs in New Orleans; namely, the inexperience and incompetence of Bob s manager, Martin Julian. Formerly part of a travelling acrobatic act with his sister Rose, Julian had befriended Bob and taken over the responsibility of managing him. In doing so, he d apparently ousted the man who d filled that role rather more capably, a former policeman named Captain Glori, a friend of the Fitzsimmons family. If Martin s skill in negotiating a winning purse for his client in New Orleans is anything to go by, he was a disaster as a manager, and perhaps should have remained on his trapeze. But there was another, more personal reason that the Cornish boxer was enjoying the rather dubious benefit of the former acrobat s services.

He may have been blessed with an extraordinary natural talent as a fighter, but not even such a renowned storyteller as Fitz himself would dare to suggest that he was possessed of any great physical beauty. Aside from the top-heavy physique which looked as if it had been manufactured from two separate bodies by a rather careless craftsman, he was lacking the clean-cut, boyish good looks of contemporaries such as James Corbett. To start with, he d lost most of his hair while still a young man, a fact which made him appear older than he actually was. Unfortunately, he was an early pioneer of the ill-advised tonsorial practice which involves combing a few strands of hair across one s otherwise bald crown. Apart from anything else, this precarious hairstyle wasn t best suited to Bob s particular profession. The strategically-placed strands would fly about madly, as his sweat-soaked head was battered here and there about the ring. He himself once said, tongue-in-cheek: In hair I have quality over quantity. It was this thinning red hair, coupled with his violently-freckled complexion, which earned him numerous nicknames in the American press. Ruby Fitz and Speckled Bob are among those which are fit to repeat here. Overall, his lean, sharp features were those of the wily, streetwise predator, while his hands had gradually been mangled beyond recognition into gnarled, mis-shapen appendages. While he dressed the part of a gentleman, expensively decked out in the finest top hats and silk cravats, he still looked for all the world like an unusually well-dressed blacksmith. Standing at just under six feet tall, and weighing in at around eleven-and-a-half stone, he was wiry and rangy — ideal for a fighter, but rather less suited as a society clothes-horse.

A writer in a leading American newspaper described him thus:

> There is nothing of the mastiff about his features . . . Rather small blue eyes, steady, but not fierce, a fair complexion, sandy-coloured hair, a receding brow made noticeable by encroaching baldness, an ordinary nose with some traces of rough usage, a square chin, and a firm-set full-lipped mouth, which in conversation reveals the inevitable gold teeth of American citizenship. Such a man is Fitzsimmons, but to this description must be added the evidence of terrific power about the man s physique.

So, we can assume the reasons for his considerable success in attracting the opposite sex were by no means immediately apparent. Certainly, at the peak of his fame, he was extremely rich. But the less cynical amongst us would say it s just as likely that the charm and charisma which had endeared him to fans across the country may also have inspired his personal relationships. The enduring love of his life was the prettier half of that Australian acrobatic duo. Although the full extent of her former high-flying skills are largely unknown it was her demeanour while on firm ground that attracted the young Cornishman, their mutual love for performing arts having conspired with fate to throw them together.

Their passionate — and secret — affair led to the break-up of Fitzsimmons s marriage to his first wife, Alice. This untidy domestic situation was soon neatly resolved, however, when Rose s brother kept it in the family by marrying the newly-divorced Alice, and bringing up young Charles Fitzsimmons as his own. This rather unorthodox arrangement caused something of a social stir in the puritanical America of the 1890s and would prove to be something of an albatross for the Cornishman to bear in later years, as Martin Julian would prove himself to be more and more spectacularly inept at controlling a professional fighter s career; although rather less backward in terms of taking his cut of any earnings which came their way. His share of Bob s prize money was believed to be up to a staggering fifty per cent — a significant factor in Fitz s future financial problems. There is no record of the entrepreneur having any previous experience in the fight game, nor even any actual interest in it. It was almost certainly his sister s influence which allowed Julian to remain part of the Fitzsimmons entourage long after he d proved himself to be surplus to useful requirements.

Rose was popularly believed to have had a far more beneficial effect on Bob s fortunes, one which went even beyond their obvious domestic contentment. There is a popular legend surrounding the former Miss Julian, who d captured the ring hero s heart so totally. This relates that it was her personal intervention, from a ringside seat, which led to her husband s 1897 world title victory, when at a crucial moment she cried: Hit im in the slats, Bob! This endearing tale of Rose s inspired coaching style has been disputed by some, who claim it s one of the many myths which thread throughout the Fitzsimmons story. In other words, possibly a figment of Mr Fitzsimmons s own imagination. Whether it s true or not, the sight of the petite, expensively-dressed lady enthusiastically voicing her support in a similarly energetic manner, was said to have been a familar one around the American boxing circuit of the time. She also formed a permanent fixture in training camps and sparring sessions where her husband carefully fine-tuned his legendary fitness, prior to important fights. In turn, Bob thought the world of his wife. He would go to unnecessarily great lengths to explain — to anyone who d listen — what a precious, shining jewel of a woman she was. He proclaimed repeatedly — and with some poetic licence — how blessed he was to have this eternal ray of sunshine brightening up his humble life. In addition to her stunning beauty and permanent sweet nature, he said, with true diplomacy, she was also a very good cook.

The ensuing years would prove to be a particularly happy time in the Fitzsimmons household — on both the personal and professional fronts. For once in Fitz s often chaotic life, things seemed to be running smoothly. The family were financially secure, thanks to his increasing public profile, and they seemed by all accounts to be genuinely content to be in each other s company. Bob would have been at ease with himself like never before, reaping the benefit of his hard-earned ringcraft and providing a standard of living for his family which most could only dream of. A lover of fine food and drink, Fitzsimmons grew accustomed to the opulence and luxury to which a gentleman of his stature was now entitled and he lived the life of a king, within his own personal kingdom.

Another factor of Bob s private life at this time provides us with a useful insight into his character. At the peak of his fame, he and his family resided in a beautiful house in the Bensonhurst area of New York — an area which now forms part of the Brooklyn district. The house was set in exquisite gardens, designed and maintained to the finest detail. No expense was spared in the decoration of the interior, with lavish ornaments and fine furnishings. It was here that luxurious guest rooms were permanently on standby to receive friends and other visitors, as the Fitzsimmons relished the role of congenial hosts. Described as charming company, they counted politicians, business people, artists, actors and other professionals among their closest accquaintances. Friends pointed out that the relaxed, witty *bon viveur* who headed the dinner table was far removed from the brutal prizefighter who was capable of killing a man with those same hands which now deftly carved the pheasant or duck. One particular guest seemed to enjoy permanent status within the household; an elderly, white-haired man who was introduced to everyone as Dr Lapraik. The true identity of the mysterious Dr Lapraik remained a closely guarded secret, until it was inadvertently discovered by an acquaintance of the couple. It finally emerged that the frail old man was none other than the owner of the blacksmith s shop in which the young Robert once worked. Having heard that his former employer had fallen on hard times, the world champion set about tracing him, as the old man was far too proud to come to him with his problems. When he finally located his old boss, Fitzsimmons sent the following message: I am on Easy Street now, old boy. Come and live with me, and take a rest in your old age!

So it was that his old friend was welcomed into the house, where he enjoyed a luxurious lifestyle beyond the wildest of his expectations. As the old man was a veterinary surgeon by profession, a workshop was immediately installed for his benefit, where he was able to amuse himself as he pleased. His financial worries were over; he now had a roof over his head for the rest of his days. It was a stark contrast from the far-off times in Australia when the young Cornish immigrant would work long hours in Dr Lapraik s forge, excusing himself for a half-day when a big fight was being staged in the area. The old man laughingly remembered how his young apprentice would deny that he was the Robert Fitzsimmons being talked about in all the sporting pages, for fear of losing his horse-shoeing job.

Another recipient of the Fitzsimmons hospitality proved to be less grateful. Bob s love for animals was well documented, with many tales circulating of his wrestling with lions and bears to stay in shape. He d apparently discovered this gift while working as a blacksmith, soothing and reassuring horses as they stood still to be re-shod. But one member of the animal kingdom which did get the better of him was a parrot he d purchased as a pet. Forever the showman, he d boasted to a writer named Robert H Davis that he was teaching the parrot to talk, and would he like to see it? Davis was intrigued enough to visit the palatial Fitzsimmons home, where he witnessed the world boxing champion slowly and patiently talking to a large, brightly-coloured macaw. Efforts to establish a reciprocal conversation proved unsuccessful, and as it was now late, the two men decided to retire for the night. Davis describes how a thunderstorm blew up over New York, with forks of lightning dramatically illuminating the room where the parrot rested on its perch. Woken in fright, it panicked, leapt into the air and took off, eventually finding its owner s bedroom in its frenzy. It landed squarely on Fitzsimmons s naked body as the boxer lay sleeping, digging its large talons into the bare flesh. Rising from the bed with a decidedly unmanly shriek, Fitzsimmons leapt from his bed and dashed through a screen door, fleeing out into the garden, where he raced — still naked — across the grass. Not to be deterred, the parrot clung on for dear life, attacking the fighter fiercely with its beak. The pair must have created quite a spectacle, as the nude boxer darted about his garden in a blind panic, with an angry bird still adorning his famous physique, refusing to let go. For once, it seemed, the fearless champion had been forced to take flight from an opponent.

The same Mr Davis was also present during another of Fitz s domestic escapades, one which would also end in tears. Davis and Fitzsimmons had returned to the Bath beach house late at night, after what we can safely assume had been an evening of fairly intensive wine-tasting. As a result, both men were in a highly jovial mood, and the champion was showing off more than ever. These high spirits led to the pair invading the kitchen in search of a midnight snack. Within a short time, Fitzsimmons was cracking eggs, throwing them into a pan with typical gusto and flair, and whipping up a large omelette as his friend looked on. There is no mention in any of his numerous press cuttings which praises his culinary talents, so we can possibly guess he wasn t in possession of any. The hearty feast Bob had planned went seriously awry when he began tossing the omelette from the pan above his head, like an over-enthusiastic chef. The split-second timing which had characterised his ring career seemed temporarily to desert him, as a mess of eggs landed on his head, much to the unrestrained hilarity of both men.

Rose, however, seems to have taken rather a dim view of such merriment in her kitchen, and dashed from the master bedroom to see what all the noise was. Steaming into the kitchen, and spying her husband coated in food and giggling helplessly, she didn t hesitate for a second. Laying into him like an experienced professional, she forcefully landed a heavy cuff on the upside of his freckled head, upon which he promptly lost his balance and crashed to the ground. Helpless with laughter, he lay there amidst the mess, while his wife stormed out of the room.

Davis, relieved that he appeared to have escaped punishment, reported that the legendary prizefighter would certainly have failed to beat a count of ten, as he lay, crying with laughter, on the kitchen floor.

It would be remembered as the night when the Fighting Blacksmith met the Fighting Butcher. This particular tradesmen s convention heralded the coming together of Bob Fitzsimmons and the Chicago-based Abe Cougle, a man whose pre-fight hype described him as the hardest hitter who d ever been discovered. This rather optimistic statement aside, the young man was certainly seen as another rigorous test for the world middleweight champion, who was proving himself to be something of a boxing oddity, in that he seemed more than happy to fight anyone who d take him on, regardless of the financial incentive or possible consequences. More cautious champions may have shuddered at such an easy-going, *laissez-faire* approach, but it merely reflected Fitzsimmons s unshakeable confidence in his own abilities. For his part, Cougle was certainly no slouch. Topping six feet four inches in height and weighing around two hundred and thirty pounds, the butcher had recently accomplished the remarkable feat of dropping four fighters in the course of one evening, with only a brief rest between each contest. It was possibly this impressive addition to his curriculum vitae that brought him to the attention of the fight promoters, desperately seeking a match for the seemingly unstoppable British fighter, whose name was the talk of all sporting circles. Their meeting would form part of a touring variety show, in which Fitzsimmons would give a demonstration of sparring, bag-punching and other training routines, before re-enacting the triumphant battle with Dempsey which had won him the world middleweight championship. Having dispensed with his tame sparring partner, he would then challenge all to get into a ring with him. The man who was still standing after four rounds would win the sum of $100.

The promoter of these events was Captain Glori, Bob s former manager. The San Francisco-based entrepreneur had been instrumental in establishing Fitz s career Stateside supporting him financially and using his theatrical contacts to capitalise on the Cornishman s growing notoriety. Cougle was lined up to join the bill of one of these shows, much to the satisfaction of those members of the audience who were aware of his reputation. The prospect of the formidably huge American battling the notoriously hard-hitting Englishman seemed to guarantee an action-packed evening. Naturally, the usual charade of ring politics had to come into play first, as Cougle was billed to fight both Jim Hall and Bob Fitzsimmons on the same evening and was forced to choose who to meet first. A good deal of soft-soaping from the persuasive Fitzsimmons convinced the young butcher that it would be in his interests to fight him, so he agreed to do so, presumably in the hope of toppling the renowned ring-battler. The man from Chicago put up a brave fight. He was big, strong and not afraid to engage his more experienced adversary in open combat. Against another opponent, he may even have made his mark. But the sad truth was, he was simply out of his depth. Fitzsimmons, the wily artiste with bags of style to match his superlative strength, was just too quick for any of Cougle s punches to gain any impact, and too slippery to become trapped in any corners. Eventually, Cougle began to tire, flailing wild punches in increasingly desperate flurries. Fitz was actually giving him an easy ride, but ironically this had the unintentional effect of frustrating the American even more. Finally — and perhaps understandably — Cougle appeared to rather lose his head somewhat. Firstly, he wrapped a meaty arm around his opponent s slight frame, pulling his upper body towards him. Then he used his considerable bulk to trap him in a headlock, as the referee tried to break them apart. As he did this, Cougle wilfully ignored the rules of the ring to deal two sharp blows to the wriggling Fitzsimmons, catching him on top of his head. The Cornishman s forehead soon began to swell where he d been hit. Aside from the discomfort, Fitzsimmons was clearly hopping mad. The gentleman s courtesy he d offered to his inexperienced opponent had been rudely rejected. It was time for the play-acting to stop. All of a sudden, the mood in the ring had changed from that of robust entertainment to one of serious intent. All niceties had been dropped.

In the next few minutes, Abe Cougle underwent a dramatic career change. He d been dealt such a severe and comprehensive beating by the enraged Fitzsimmons that a future in boxing s top flight was becoming a more remote possibility with every moment that passed. The gulf between the two was glaringly wide, and growing ever larger. As Speckled Bob punched with heart-stopping speed and accuracy, his hits pounding their exposed targets one after another, Cougle seemed rooted to the spot, his defences in tatters. Despite the vast difference in size, he found himself totally at the champion s mercy, his head jarring under one bone-crunching blow after another, as he desperately tried to duck below the oncoming missiles. It was a question of pedigree — judging by this display alone, Fitzsimmons was now truly a world-class contender, while Cougle would only ever be an also-ran. The one-sided spectacle finally ceased moments later, as a right-handed swing slammed into the side of Cougle s drooping head, sending him spinning to the floor, where he slowly rolled over, and then remained motionless.

Cougle was carried unconscious to the dressing room, where doctors worked for more than half an hour to revive him. The scheduled fight with Hall was cancelled. He would never enter the ring again.

The following day, Fitzsimmons was resting at his hotel, allowing his body to relax after the vigours of the previous night s workout. This was a luxury which was only afforded him occasionally, as the schedules of travelling and performing left him little or no idle time. He was still getting used to the pressure of fame, although the five-star treatment and public adulation was hardly a serious concern, compared to hammering countless horseshoes in a steaming-hot forge. As he lay contentedly on his soft bed, one of his companions burst into the room shouting at the top of his voice. He was in a panic and tried to usher the startled boxer out onto the metal fire escape. When questioned on the whereabouts of the fire, he breathlessly explained the reason for the fuss. It s worse than a fire — it s hell let loose! he babbled. Cougle s four brothers are downstairs, and they re going to get even with you for the slugging you gave the butcher last night! Fitz didn t seem unduly concerned. If each of them is only as good at fighting as Cougle is, I ll beat the whole family with my left hand tied behind my back, he observed, showing true characteristic modesty. Bravado aside, it s likely the Cornishman actually meant what he said, as his fighting spirit was never far from the surface. His friend paled at such a rough-handed notion. No you can t, Fitz — don t be such a fool! You don t know what they might do . . . they might have their butchers knives with them! Bob considered this possibility for a moment. Ever the master of the understatement, he ventured: Well, when I see what they have, that may be the time to think about getting a move on.

As Fitzsimmons walked out into the hallway, brushing aside all protests, a full-scale riot was on the point of breaking out as porters, clerks, waiters and bellboys tried to eject the four large men in their midst. Someone called from the m l e: Get back into your room, Mr Fitzsimmons — the Cougle brothers are here! The crowd parted as the fighter walked towards the men. Regular followers of his fights would have recognised the stance he adopted, as he prepared himself for the physical conflict which seemed about to manifest itself. The tension of the moment was immediately broken, however, when the largest of the four men turned to him and spoke in a calm voice. Smiling, he said, gently: We have come to congratulate you, Mr Fitzsimmons! Noting the puzzled looks around him, he continued: You did something last night that we as an entire family have been trying to do for the last six years, but unsuccessfully. Enjoying his audience s undivided attention, he went on: We have nothing against fighting as a business, but we want every member of our family to be in the butcher business, and so we are very much opposed to Abe and his championship aspirations, but you have killed any thought of ambition in that direction, and Abe is back again today, doing what we have all been doing all our lives.

It must have taken a certain amount of bravery to approach the world middleweight boxing champion in this way; and the happy ending to the episode sealed a firm friendship between the Cougle and Fitzsimmons families which continued for a long time afterwards. It s likely that some choice cuts of meat made their way to the Fitzsimmons home over the next few years.

Why was Fitz such a good fighter?

It seems highly improbable — outside the realms of improbable action-hero movies — that a strangely-built, balding blacksmith, well past the first flush of youth, would have been capable of physically overpowering the biggest and best fighters that the entire United States of America could produce. Huge, brawny men were ignominiously despatched to the canvas; hardened prizefighters were thoroughly bruised and battered before finally falling at the great man s feet. The Fighting Blacksmith not only worked out with the tools of his former trade — a hammer and anvil — in order to tone his peak-condition body even further; but also continued to hone his lethal finishing power by smashing hardened turnips into pieces with his bare hands. Even during contests where the opponent could put up rather more of a fight than that of the turnip, Fitzsimmons s endurance almost always proved to be the more lasting of the two, ending in the predictably one-sided result.

What was his secret? How could this man, standing just over five feet eleven inches, and weighing barely twelve stone, whip every battle-hardened brawler from New Orleans to New York?

The answer almost certainly lay in a combination of his speed, power and technique. All were important components which, when combined, served up a potent cocktail of blurring attack and blistering force. Experts of the time claimed that Fitzsimmons was possessed with a strong punch unleashing it as he did with such deadly effect. His deftness and agility in a ring were unequalled, while he used his smaller frame to skilfully avoid the punches of bigger, slower men. His technique was both scientific and instinctive; analysing opponents and devising his ring tactics accordingly, using his observations to predict how the other man would behave, and counteracting their moves in the way a military leader would play on the weaknesses of an opposing army. But it was his streetwise instinct which married all of these together in mortal combat. He was possessed of a sixth sense telling him when to defend and when to attack, when to tire his opponent and when to go in for the kill. His fighting was that of a predatory creature that knows the exact moment in which to swoop on its prey.

Showcased in a straight-backed, almost imperious stance, drawn from the copybook of old-fashioned bare-knuckle sideshows, Fitzsimmons s upper body gave the appearance of having been quarried from the granite of his native Cornwall. The lightness of his footwork would keep his bobbing head safely out of range from the reaches of the roughneck giants who could only follow in his wake. The same giants were invariably stopped in those same tracks, when a blurring left hook would arc from the lithe torso which danced before them. It was in this way that many a fearsome-looking warrior was pole-axed. It was in this way that many a proud fighter was humbly reduced to his hands and knees by the superior skills of his opponent. Fitz was said by many to combine this easy, artistic grace with a cast-iron strength. He was like an iron fist in a velvet glove. The way in which he harnessed this white-hot energy made him one of the most entertaining ring performers of all time.

His early fights, in the days when bare knuckles and dirt-floor rings were yet to give way to gloves and canvas, always ended swiftly and abruptly. In later years a well-aimed left hand would still send the biggest and most menacing bully into a sudden, deep sleep. He called it his left-hand shift —the fast feinting with his right hand, which cleared his opponent s guard, only for a lethal missile to meet its target. He once said that his power did not come from his arm, but was generated by his entire body. He explained:

> In every story written by the average novelist, the hero always knocks down the villain with a blow straight from the shoulder.

PRIZE FIGHTER

No professional boxer hits like that. The blow, in order to be effective, comes right up from the feet. Every muscle of the body plays its part. When I hit, the muscles on my chest — the pectoral muscles — pull my shoulder forward. The muscles behind my shoulder push it forward. Every muscle up my back, from my waist, swings the weight of my body onto the blow.

Having explained the technique, he went on to outline the consequences: Hitting like that, I can knock a man out, if my hand has three inches play from the time it starts, to the time it strikes my man. The result of such a blow is that he feels as though he has been hit by the actual explosion — not by the bullets. Men such as Peter Maher and Jack Dempsey would almost certainly testify to this. Fitz once described his talents thus: I have been told that I am about the hardest hitter that ever lived. At any rate, I have done enough hitting in my time to know something about it. From anyone else, this may have seemed like pure bragging, but his ring record suggests otherwise: 369 fights over a thirty-one-year career with around two hundred of them ending within the first two rounds. In later years, he would be elected to the International Boxing Hall of Fame with fight expert Charley Rose ranking him as the greatest light heavyweight fighter of all time. Modern-day records still describe him as one of the greatest fighters that ever lived. The secrets of Fitzsimmons s success were outlined in a book penned by the man himself, entitled *Physical Culture and Self-Defence*. Published in 1901, it included such techniques as Right-Hand Counter and Block , Foul Pivotal Blow and The Slip — Resorted To In The Face of Threatened Punishment . If any of Fitzsimmons s future opponents managed to read this pugilist s Bible, however, they would seem to have failed, in the main, to take its contents on board. The book s introduction, which was written by AJ Drexel Biddle, described its author as this most wonderful of fighters . He went on: In his most recent victories, Fitzsimmons has done more for the cause of scientific boxing, the manly art of self-defence, than any other person has ever accomplished . . . By his victories, he clearly proved that superior science is more than a match for superior size and strength, even with youth to back such desirable qualities. Though a word must be said about Fitzsimmons s physique, for he is, indeed, a man of iron.

It was this very physique which was sufficiently admired to become a permanent fixture in New York, with the erection of a statue at Dewey Arch, which was fashioned by the local sculptor DC French. So it was that when Admiral Dewey received his great ovation in New York, it was Helston s most famous son, Robert James Fitzsimmons, who looked expressionlessly down at him, from his plinth, eighteen feet from the ground. *Physical Culture and Self Defence* wasn t the veteran boxer s only foray into the world of print. The year of 1909, when the sun was fast setting on his days in the ring, saw him trying his hand as a journalist, with a series of autobiographical articles for the *Sunday Dispatch* newspaper. They gave an intimate, highly personal account of some of his most notorious ring-battles, from Tom Sharkey to James Corbett. The memoirs are both lucid and entertaining, as he re-lived the highs and lows of his remarkable life. The most telling insights into his philosophical outlook at the age of forty-six are those which frankly analyse the calling which made him a household name. He wrote in one article: Today I wouldn t walk across the street to see a contest, and nothing but the request of some friend to second him in the ring would ever make me see a fight again. To fight 369 battles of your own is enough to take any feeling of pleasure in fighting for its own sake out of you.

It seemed the old stager had lost his taste for battle, with the many years of punishment taking their toll on his appetite for boxing as a spectacle. He may well have simply become disillusioned with a sport which had to all intents and purposes left him behind, in search of new, younger champions.

Back when Robert Fitzsimmons was first beginning to make a name for himself with his colourful showmanship and spectacular fighting skills, another man was starting his own ascendancy to the ranks of boxing s prized inner circle. While their paths had already crossed briefly, that other man would soon carve his own niche into the consciousness of the sporting nation, and he would become, above all others, the Cornishman s lifelong nemesis. James Corbett was born in San Francisco in 1866 into a family of Irish immigrants, who would raise twelve children in the country which they now called home. His father supported the family by means of a successful livery stables business. After leaving school, young James worked as a clerk, later taking a good job in a local bank. A comfortable, middle-class lifestyle would have been beckoning, had not the attractions of the famous Olympic Boxing Club proved far stronger. Proving himself to be an elegant fighter of extreme cleverness and sharp-thinking, he applied science to his clashes, using supreme grace and wily skill in out-manoeuvring and outwitting his opponents. To a calling born in the backstreet pool-halls and disreputable bar-rooms, Corbett represented a welcome breath of fresh air; a fine, upstanding young man who embraced middle-American values and competed fairly and honourably. More than any other boxer of his age, he was responsible for introducing an entirely different element to prizefight audiences, helping to popularise the image of the sport and significantly broaden its appeal as it approached the twentieth century. This is one of the reasons that so many men of the day — Fitzsimmons included — who earned a living by hitting other men for money, are often pictured in top hats and suits. Apparently craving respect-ability, they yearned to be thought of as gentlemen.

This progressive attitude was, of course, totally at odds with old-fashioned street sluggers such as John L Sullivan. Corbett s comparatively well-to-do background was also in sharp contrast to the likes of Fitzsimmons, who d learned to fight competitively in the era of dusty prize rings and open-air bareknuckle contests. Nevertheless, Corbett enjoyed great popularity among an American public always on the lookout for homegrown heroes. They christened him Gentleman Jim in tribute to his renowned charm and general deportment. Admittedly, when compared against toughs such as Sailor Tom Sharkey, with his cauliflower ears and tattoos, or Jim Jeffries, with his combative, streetfighter attitude, the term of gentleman wasn t difficult to come by. It would have been very tempting for other journeyman brawlers in the country to attempt to permanently rearrange Corbett s boyish looks. It says much for his superlative skills with the gloves that none was successful in this aim. An early bout against the fast-hitting Joe Choynski, which was staged out of the police s reach aboard a floating barge, ended in the twenty-seventh round, when serious facial injuries inflicted forced Choynski to quit. The loser on that occasion fared little better in the re-match, which ended after only four rounds, with the same result.

But it was only when he faced the famed Boston Strong Boy (Sullivan s self-appointed title) that Corbett s personal stock really began to increase in value. On paper, a contest between a hard-living, hard-swearing barbarian and a young, clean-cut former bank clerk could only have one outcome, but two factors would greatly influence the result. Corbett was in his physical and mental prime, working hard and preparing meticulously for each battle, working out his opponent s tactical failings in order to fully exploit them to his advantage. Secondly, Sullivan was slightly past his personal sell-by date, having enjoyed rather too much good living and not nearly enough good training. As a result, Sullivan was emphatically cut down to size by the deceptively baby-faced challenger, and a new world champion was born. The older, bulkier man had been left breathless by the hectic pace of the contest, which finished with him receiving a good deal of punishment; yet being unable to fight back, through a combination of fatigue and pain. It was Corbett s turn to enjoy the high life, appearing on the theatrical stage in the melodrama *Gentleman Jack* and reaping the benefits of his new-found celebrity. He soon enjoyed a devoted fan following, and not only because of his prowess with his fists. He cut a dashing figure, with his neatly combed hair and snappy dress style, and he enjoyed playing the role of the swashbuckling aesthete.

To all appearances, Corbett may have seemed more like a movie star than a boxer, and this calling actually materialised on 8 September 1894. A bout between Corbett and a man named Peter Courtney, of Trenton, New Jersey, became the first-ever prizefight to be filmed. The machine used was a Kinetoscope, invented by the renowned Thomas Edison. The camera contained within it was a Kinetograph, which was capable of recording moving images onto fifty-foot loops of film. The device was first used in public on 14 April 1894, when people queued round the block to witness this miracle of the modern day. Each kinetoscope production lasted no more than a minute, and — something of a drawback — could only be viewed by one person at a time in its earliest days.

Nevertheless, the celebrated occasion which would permanently preserve the handsome visage of James Corbett in cinematic history took place at the Edison Laboratory in New Jersey, in a specially-built structure known as a Black Maria. This was actually a tiny, primitive version of a film studio, measuring only fifteen feet wide. Looking rather like a sinister armoured tank from the outside, the Black Maria let in the strong sunlight which was necessary for the equipment to capture the action. The walls of the space were padded on two sides up to a height of six feet, while ropes were set up between the walls to set out a ring. As the sun moved, the whole structure had to be shifted, so that the images could once again be illuminated. Each round could only last a minute and a half, before the film would run out. The heat would have made the sweat-box conditions inside almost unbearable. Amazingly, with all these bizarre, new-fangled happenings going on around them, the two fighters managed to conduct something resembling a proper contest in this way, with Corbett knocking Courtney out cold in the sixth round. Ironically, after all that trouble, the films were never shown. When he was persuaded to tear himself away from his adoring public and once more trouble himself with stepping into a ring, the clean-cut idol gave British bare-knuckle champion Charley Mitchell such a thrashing that the Englishman must have regretted stepping into it himself. Like others before and since, Corbett continued combining his first profession with that of treading the highly-lucrative boards of vaudeville.

As we ve heard, the name of Fitzsimmons had been raucously brought to the Irishman s attention by means of that irrepressible character having the gall to loudly issue a challenge to the champion of a far heavier weight division. This obviously offended Corbett s rather more refined sensibilities, as he frequently denounced Fitzsimmons as an uncouth, loudmouthed braggart, who had the mother of all beatings coming to him. Corbett was generally seen as a legitimate successor to the Boston Strong Boy, and, as such, was a natural rival for Fitzsimmons, who fancied his own chances against the Californian. For his turn, the loud-mouthed braggart told the press and public at every available opportunity that he would take on the Irish-American wherever and whenever he liked; even in the street, if necessary. This exchange, and the many more which were to follow, were greedily seized upon by the journalistic birds of prey — those headline-seeking papermen promoting the newly-popular sport to a public hungry for heroes. If all this huffing and puffing sounds like idle boasting, subsequent events would prove it was anything but. By pure co-incidence, both men were appearing in stage plays in the city of Philadelphia during the summer of 1895. The two men met by chance in the lobby of a top-class hotel. Corbett rushed over to Fitz and confronted him, asking if he was looking for trouble. He then grabbed the Cornishman by the nose, where upon a violent struggle ensued.

The scene is one from a movie set — two well-dressed, affluent men; one the world heavyweight boxing champion, the other holding the equivalent middleweight title — cursing and brawling like a pair of drunks in a roadhouse parking lot. The fact that both men were more than capable of inflicting mortal injury with their fists turned the scenario from farcical comedy to high drama. Everyone had seen both of them in action — it didn t take much imagination to foresee what could happen if they were left to slug it out between themselves. Luckily, responsible grown-ups were on hand, in the form of Corbett s brother Joe and several hotel staff, to break up the potentially disastrous fight. Next day, the press related the incident in all its salacious detail, gleefully proclaiming that two of America s top professional fighters had come close to staging an impromptu bare-knuckle scrap, in the ornate lobby of a prestigious hotel. It would have done little to calm the authorities long-held concerns over prizefighting and even less to confirm either man s dignity or reputation. In true schoolyard style each claimed the other had started it. Fitzsimmons claimed that Corbett had outrageously insulted the very essence of his manhood by tweaking his nose, while Corbett claimed Fitz had deliberately come to the hotel where he was staying with the express intention of picking a fight. As if that wasn t bad enough, a further incident served only to inflame their animosity further. Tentative plans had been laid for the two to meet. A bloodthirsty public fairly salivated at the prospect of what was sure to be a supremely ill-tempered grudge match.

A fight was arranged and various venues considered. The high-profile couple found it difficult to find an arena in which to slug out their differences. On one occasion the fight was due to take place in Texas, but the authorities got wind of the scheme, and threatened to place heavy fines on any promoter who would consider staging such wickedness in the Lone Star State. Another plan to hold the bout in the neighbouring state of Arkansas led to both Corbett and Fitzsimmons being arrested during the run-up to the event and charged with conspiring to commit a breach of the peace. The two fighters were bailed on a behaviour bond and told to leave Arkansas forthwith. If relations between the two had been hostile before, they must have been made worse by such a fiasco, with both suffering inconvenience and a loss of prize money, not to mention the public humiliation of being treated like common criminals. Although history doesn t recall, it s assumed that while waiting to appear before the magistrate, the two arch-rivals weren t held in the same cell, for reasons of security. Corbett would play a central role in Fitzsimmons s story as both men continued to enjoy the ever-increasing wealth and glamour of their celebrity lifestyles. Much to Fitzsimmons s undoubted annoyance, Corbett was feted as one of the most popular world champions of the time and held up as a shining example of this new breed of sportsman.

If Corbett s dandyish image had raised doubts about his ability to go all the way in a brutal, all-out contest, that fight with Sullivan at New Orleans must surely have quelled those fears. The ageing Sullivan was led a merry dance by the former clerk, missing punches and swinging in vain at his darting opponent. For his part, Corbett swung some savage thrusts into Sullivan s bear-like head, knocking the older man back with short, jarring jabs. After one hour and twenty minutes, the fight was stopped, and the day of this most infamous of prizefighters was effectively at an end. There was no room in the modern sport for hulking dinosaurs like Sullivan. Men of his generation who lived through the bare-knuckle era regarded this as the death knell of their own art, and grumbled that fighting had lost its edge. Certainly, it had lost one of its greatest characters. In later years, Corbett became an ambassador for boxing, trading on his whiter-than-white public image to good effect, whilst maintaining his profile by contributing to a number of newspapers and sporting publications.

At the close of his career, however, the sheen which had traditionally covered his onstage persona took on a distinctly tarnished look when he was accused of cheating in a bout staged in New York. During a fight with Sailor Tom Sharkey, the two fighters were swapping blows when one of Corbett s seconds, a man named Connie McVey, climbed through the ropes, mid-round. This caused referee John Kelly to declare a foul and award the fight to Sharkey, stating that all bets were off. There was a public outcry, with newspapers and punters claiming that the event had been fixed. Corbett appeared to survive the scandal, however, as nothing was ever proved, and the investigation was later dropped.

He led a comfortable life of comparatively sedate retirement, dabbling with theatrical shows and public engagements. He eventually died at his New York home in 1933 at the age of sixty-seven, having been diagnosed with cancer. Two decades later, his life would be immortalised in the Hollywood film *Gentleman Jim*, which related the story of his glamorous rise to fame. Another famous swashbuckling character would take the lead role — an actor named Errol Flynn.

6. Duel in the Desert

Langtry, Texas
1896

One of the most celebrated incidents in the colourful life and times of Robert Fitzsimmons centred on a small town in Texas, not far from the Mexican border. The story reads rather like a script for a cowboy movie, albeit a rather far-fetched one, with a cast of cowboys and Indians, Texas Rangers and hobo gamblers. The episode inspired a book, Dan Stuart s *Fistic Carnival*, featuring a number of the many larger-than-life characters which have since become associated with the Wild West thrown together in a situation which was, to say the least, bizarre.

Formed from the counties of Kinney, Crockett and the Pecos, Val Verde was officially established as a county in the year 1885. Covering more than three thousand square miles, the territory was, at that time, a largely uninhabited plain in the south-west corner of the Lone Star state. Mile after mile of desert was occasionally interrupted by small, shanty-like towns, consisting of a few tumbledown shacks. A local authority was clearly needed to administer law and order across the area, as pockets of the West were still relatively wild in those last few years of the nineteenth century. Official records from that time tell us that the man elected to serve in that proud capacity, upholding the laws of the United States to the best of his ability, was a man named Roy Bean. A rough diamond, the newly appointed Justice of the Peace re-christened himself Judge Roy Bean, in keeping with his lofty status. It s a name which has featured largely in books, movies and TV shows ever since. Bean installed himself in a small corner of the county, effectively creating his own town, which expanded in direct relation to its founder s burgeoning reputation. Experts in modern

American history relate that the sheer force of his personality was in fact the key to the town s rapid growth. The new development was christened Langtry, a typically subtle homage to the object of the Judge s desires, the English actress Lillie Langtry. (Unfortunately, it seems this love remained unrequited. Bean asked Langtry several times to visit his little kingdom, but by all accounts, she somehow managed to resist his unique charm.)

In countless Western movies, the new sheriff has to gain control of a town by brawling, shooting and otherwise gently persuading the inhabitants to come round to his way of thinking. It s likely that Bean was the original inspiration for this unorthodox brand of local government, as he was said to have ruled with the proverbial iron hand. He dispensed this justice from an extremely seedy-looking saloon which served as a combination of bar, billiard hall, courtroom and jail. Incidentally, the famous Jersey Lily Saloon is still standing, almost a century after the passing of its most famous landlord — it has long since become a popular tourist landmark. Where the Judge once sentenced cattle rustlers to swing on the end of a rope for their crimes, camera-toting European tourists now queue to buy souvenir pens and postcards. If Bean s thinking on law and order wasn t the most liberal, it was at least relatively straightforward. Anyone considered by the Judge to be straying from his personal path of righteousness was summarily beaten up, shot or both; this was all done in the hope that other potentially lawless elements would be suitably discouraged. Perhaps unsurprisingly, this rather draconian method of law enforcement actually seemed to work. The irrepressible hoodlum thus became known as The Law, West of the Pecos , or The Hanging Judge , and if higher authorities disapproved of his methods, they seemed reasonably happy to let him get on with it, just as long as he didn t cause too much trouble. With parts of Texas still suffering from an over-abundance of trigger-happy outlaws, it s likely they may have had rather more important things to think about at the time. As stories of the Judge s many adventures began to spin across the West, so legends began to take root. As well as eventually being portrayed by Paul Newman in a Hollywood film, the great man has also been latterly immortalised in the Judge Roy Bean Visitor

PRIZE FIGHTER

Center, which stands proudly in the town of Langtry today, for those same snap-happy tourists to take in during their visit.

Back in 1896, it was this very fame which reached the ears of an enterprising group of fight promoters. The local authorities tended to take a dim view of prizefighting at that time — it was illegal in most states, although it was actually tolerated unofficially in many. Fights staged in secret, remote locations attracted fair-sized crowds, who were obviously drawn by the spectacle of undiluted violence. In order for a major, high-profile fight to be staged, a suitable public venue needed to be found. After all, men who were prepared to bet hundreds of dollars on the outcome of such a bout wouldn t have taken kindly to tramping for miles through open prairieland. Where better to stage such a fight than the freewheeling Western town of Langtry, Texas? The Judge was known to be an enthusiastic fight fan, having been actively involved in quite a few himself over the years; and he was sure to throw his considerable weight behind the ambitious project. And so he did, to the extent of appointing himself co-promoter and unofficial PR man for the event, which would pit Robert Fitzsimmons against Irishman Peter Maher. Modern-day tourism experts may question the wisdom of using an illegal prizefight to advertise the attractions of a town, but Bean had no such moral qualms. With his blessing, the fight was duly arranged.

However, the Texan authorities did harbour grave concerns about the event Bean was organising, not least of which was the prospect of thousands of outlaws, cowboys, labourers and Lord knows who else besides, shattering the relative peace and quiet of Val Verde. But economic necessity prevailed. Bars, brothels and gambling houses were likely to see an upturn in trade, but this presumably was hardly the sort of trade that state dignitaries were keen to welcome. Bean was seemingly unperturbed by this opposition, although he did take the gallant measure of hiring security to protect the fighters. This security arrived in the formidable form of one William Barclay Masterson, formerly of Dodge City, Kansas. The murderous quick-draw gunman, better known as Black Bat , was joined by six of his similarly-disposed colleagues. Masterson, who was a close friend of fellow boxing enthusiast Wyatt Earp, had been drafted in to keep the crowds under control on the day itself, while ensuring the safety of both participants.

We can safely assume that those discerning fight fans who descended on Langtry and surrounding districts would have been unlikely to absorb much of the local culture, unless you counted that of the alcoholic or sexual variety. The phrase rough and ready is possibly an understatement when referring to the band of drunken ne er-do-wells who descended on this sleepy corner of Texas: their minds set on women and whisky. We can only imagine the rowdy scenes of an evening spent carousing in Langtry, as itinerant workers from cattle-ranges and copper-mines across the West travelled in on a long and dusty trail, in search of the famed prizefight. Among these numbers was a large contingent of ex-patriot miners from Cornwall who d taken time off from their new employment to enthusiastically cheer on their countryman and possibly even risk a small wager on him. The contest was taking on a truly international flavour, as any loyalty for their host country would almost certainly have been forgotten amid all the fever-pitched excitement. The arrival of the Cornish army would have represented an added bonus for the fight s promoter Dan Stuart— a 19th-century version of Don King, whose vision of professional fighting as a spectator sport with wide mass appeal was ahead of its time. The divided loyalties of the crowd would give that extra charge to the atmosphere when the fighters finally faced each other in the ring.

Unfortunately, the first sign of warfare happened — perhaps predictably — even before the first official punch was thrown. The protagonists in this pre-fight dust-up were none other than Fitzsimmons and Bean, who d clashed over that old chestnut — money. Fitzsimmons was adamant that he was being horrendously short-changed, especially as there were plans afoot to film the fight on one of the new cine-cameras. He blamed the promoters for denying him what was rightfully his, and, in characteristic style, jumped in with both feet, angrily confronting Bean in his saloon. Obviously unused to his authority being challenged so brazenly, Bean clearly didn t share the Cornishman s views on the general distribution of wealth and told him so in what we can guess was a blunt and forthright fashion. It s likely the Cornish boxer and the Texas lawman would have come to blows there and then, but instead, Bean coolly brandished a six-gun under Fitzsimmons s nose, leaving him in no doubt as to what would happen if he caused any more aggravation. Fitz may have been foolhardy, but he wasn t stupid. He knew he would have to fight. The episode can t have done much to ease his peace of mind as the day drew nearer; indeed, he had already expressed his reservations about the nature of the contest, and the unorthodox circumstances in which it was being fought.

The Texas authorities were desperate to prevent the fight from taking place, even going so far as to send state rangers to investigate its likely whereabouts. The actual location was being kept a secret by Bean and his cohorts, however, with last-minute directions to be distributed among those who d come to watch. Fitzsimmons later recounted: When the day of the fight came, we had to travel thousands of miles to get away from the rangers, who were shadowing us all over the place, and who would have stopped the fight if they possibly could. In fact, the event was causing political reverberations across the entire country. Many feared the waves of lawlessness were likely to lap over into neighbouring states, with outlaws running amok amongst decent, God-fearing folk. The matter was made worse by the already fragile state of law and order in this volatile area. The US Congress were absolutely furious from governors right up to the President himself. Some arrests were made, as pockets of minor crime threatened to get out of hand. Wrong-doers were chased across town and locked up, while sermons were preached from New York to California, as right-minded folk threw up their hands in horror at this festival of wrong-doing. Placing the event in historical context may help us to understand why the authorities were so prickly about the whole affair. America s war with the Indians actually ended that same year, when the great Apache chief Geronimo finally surrendered. Clearly, life out West hadn t exactly been a bed of roses of late.

With this in mind, reinforcements were called for; militias were summoned, and the Texas Rangers were given orders to shoot on sight. Bat Masterson summed up the feeling within Langtry when he said, All this commotion which has been stirred up because two men are going to box with five-ounce gloves seems to me to be utterly ridiculous. Unfortunately, the moral majority across the United States were hardly likely to have taken spiritual advice from one of Wyatt Earp s most notorious former gunmen, so his words of reason went largely unheeded. In fact, the necessity for his presence there seemed only to underline the seriousness of the situation. If anyone thought the adverse publicity would keep people away, they were very much mistaken. Trains groaning with their loads of professional gamblers constantly rumbled across desert plains, heading for what would surely be one of the biggest betting sprees of all time.

Oblivious to the widespread havoc they were causing, the promoters pressed on with arrangements for the fight itself. Peter Maher was cheerful about his prospects of victory, although he must have known that he was only taking part because James Corbett had washed his hands of such a sorry affair. Having narrowly survived with his life last time they d met professionally (he d swallowed blood when the inside of his mouth was torn by Fitzsimmons s fists and had almost choked to death), Maher was among a growing number of professional fighters with a score to settle. The hulking Irishman certainly couldn t be described as one of life s victims. A burly brawler whose family originally hailed from Galway, he was well-known as a powerful heavyweight slugger. Well-versed in the fistic art, the moustached giant was said to pack a lethal punch, being described as one of the hardest hitters ever to enter the squared circle. Between 1891 and 1907, he would take on the best men in the business, so highly was he rated by those in the know. As a result, betting was fairly evenly distributed in the run-up to the main attraction.

Photographs taken at ringside which have survived the passage of time paint a dramatic scene, straight from a Hollywood western, with cowboy-hatted spectators spread far and wide across the barren desert plain which surrounded the ring. With the banks of the Rio Grande providing an epic backdrop, the spectacle being promised would involve the two men fighting it out until one was unable to continue. This was a contest of sheer physical supremacy at its most raw and basic. The excitement of the occasion seemed to have overcome the famous Judge, who d been celebrating his town s newly-won place in sporting history by getting extremely drunk. He staggered into the ring prior to the main event, and slurred: This is a great day for lil ol Langtry . . . After a further series of noisy interruptions to the fight preparations, he was told to sit on a stool in a corner of the ring and behave himself. The telling moment came. At last, it was time for the warriors to take up arms. As the crowd s excitement reached fever pitch, Maher and Fitzsimmons came together in the square of dirt which had been crudely roped off into a ring. Cautiously, they began circling one another like wary predators. The Irishman s imposing presence, matched with the Cornish blacksmith s extraordinary speed and skill. Like a medieval duel, this would decide once and for all who could call himself the king. A clash of the titans being played out in the heat of the Texas desert.

As it turned out, it was actually nothing of the sort. In keeping with the farcical nature of proceedings so far, the fight was over within ninety seconds flat. The tension which had been building in Langtry for so many days and weeks finally exploded in everyone s faces. Chaos reigned for several minutes, as officials and spectators struggled to take in what had happened. A whipping left-hand punch from Fitzsimmons felled the Irishman like a dead tree. He d hit Maher so hard that he d immediately knocked him senseless. The beaten challenger lay motionless in the tinder-dry dust, the victim of a classic mismatch, which once again belied the difference in size. The Irishman had tried to foul Fitz, grabbing his neck in a deliberate move designed to exploit his own weight advantage, while punching at the same time. This cynical — and illegal — move was immediately punished, with Maher being soundly thumped into unconsciousness by the angry champion. The unlucky cameraman who d been detailed to provide worldwide syndication of the event failed lamentably in his task, as he was apparently unable to get his camera going in such a short time. Thus we are denied the privilege of viewing this sporting spectacle today. History doesn t relate the immediate reaction of Bean and the promoters. We can safely guarantee the reaction of those visiting Cornish miners.

Afterwards, Fitzsimmons boldly claimed the result of the contest had been guaranteed, and not just by the fact of him being the superior fighter. He related an incident which occurred during the men s training schedule, which he regarded as an important omen. Both camps had been set up in Warris, Mexico, where their stay happened to coincide with the Governor s Day festival. Maher and Fitzsimmons were the guests of honour at a bullfight held in the town. The first bull was to be killed in honour of the Governor, the second in honour of Fitzsimmons, and the third in honour of Maher. The Cornishman couldn t resist the chance to make mischief. He told Maher: If my bull is killed quicker than your bull, you shall win our fight; but if your bull is killed quicker than mine, I will win. Maher s reaction to this isn t recorded, but Fitzsimmons himself related that Maher s bull was killed within seconds, while Fitzsimmons s animal defeated all the bullfighters and lived to fight another day. If there was ever a metaphor to match Fitzsimmons s fighting spirit — that was it!

7. A Showdown with Wyatt Earp

14 December 1896
San Francisco, USA

The dark, hooded eyes which had once stared down countless gun barrels were now glinting angrily at the assembled reporters—many of whom had already been shuffling uneasily in the great man s presence. Instead of facing armed outlaws, the living legend of the Old West was currently squaring up to a rather more cerebral adversary — the gentlemen of the American press. Broad-brimmed hats were tipped low as heads bent forward and pencils furiously scribbled every word uttered as the hacks hid behind their notebooks. The newsmen busily avoiding the hard-eyed stare of their subject could scarcely believe the story he was relating. A succession of flash-bulbs on large, bulky box-cameras illuminated the stern profile, capturing the historic moment for posterity. It didn t take much imagination to picture the ageing gentleman in front of them. Back in his heyday the infamous Wyatt Earp would be etched in the minds of most Americans. Those were the not-so-far-off days when the West really was wild and Earp was vigorously dispensing law and order in the towns of Tombstone, Arizona and Dodge City, Kansas. His methods were direct — he d gunned down some of America s most feared outlaws in a series of bloody shoot-outs. None was more infamous than the gunfight at the OK Corral. The very same legend was now on the defensive; holding forth in the ornate wood-panelled lobby of a San Francisco hotel, his voice cracking as he tried to keep his anger in check. Gentlemen, he said. No man on earth has ever questioned my honour. I have been in many places and in many peculiar situations, but no-one ever said before tonight that I was guilty of a dishonest act. Furiously fingering the black hat on his lap, he again glared balefully at the press corps, his lips pursed tightly behind his handlebar moustache; as if daring any of those present to doubt his word. An awkward silence greeted his outburst, as the assembled reporters contemplated the full implications of what they were hearing. For the first time ever, Wyatt Earp was on the wrong side of the law he d so often risked his life to uphold. The episode has been described by Earp s biographers as casting a shadow over his reputation for integrity, which stayed with him for years to come.

The city of San Francisco was about to achieve a new claim to fame — it had been chosen as the venue for what promised to be one of the most keenly fought prizefights ever staged. Sailor Tom Sharkey, the burly ex-seaman, would take on Cornishman Bob Ruby Robert Fitzsimmons, the hard-hitting former blacksmith. It was a duel which pitted brute strength against skilful ringcraft, hard-won experience against youthful exuberance. It was also a highly illegal activity, which would have to be staged without the knowledge of the San Francisco Police Department. At first sight, odds seemed to be stacked overwhelmingly in favour of the burly Irishman. Not only did he boast a hulking, barrel-chested physique which appeared to have been carved from stone; but his savage, steamrolling aggression was that of an out-of-control bar-room brawl or alleyway streetfight. Opponents were trampled beneath his wrecking-ball approach, their bodies and spirits broken by the explosive blows he unleashed in the ring. Sharkey had learned to fight while stationed at a US naval base in Honolulu and on leaving the service he turned professional. Now based here in the Bay Area, he d already battered several seasoned professionals out of the ring in a series of brutal displays. In the rough and ready world of the 19th-century sailor, Sharkey proved that he was more than capable of looking after himself. His brawny physique was set off with an intricate tattoo of a ship, which expanded across his barrel chest, while his features bore the scars of earlier encounters, with a much-broken nose, and part of one ear missing. It was a brave man who d challenge him to step outside a saloon to settle a dispute, and an extremely foolhardy one who d dare to follow up such a challenge. Despite this, Fitzsimmons appeared to have no qualms about accepting the gauntlet so readily thrown down by the former seaman.

For this particular clash, which would take place at the

PRIZE FIGHTER

Mechanics Pavilion, San Francisco, a $10,000 purse was on offer — the winner of the ten-round contest would take it all. But the loser would risk far more than his night s pay packet. This would be a conflict which would test each man s stomach for a fight, just as much as the extent of his physical prowess. The man who won would be the man who wanted it most. With so much at stake no quarter was likely to be given on either side. It was billed as a contest for the heavyweight championship of the world — the latest in a line of mammoth battles between the mighty giants of the sport. The bookmakers — those traditionally cautious students of fight form — had weighed up Sharkey s well-documented strength against Fitzsimmons s growing reputation, and appeared to favour the latter. The consensus of opinion among gamblers of the day was that the British fighter had a fair chance of taming the rough-and-ready sailor, always assuming he was able to avoid those flailing iron fists. Talk in the many saloons and gambling houses scattered across the San Francisco waterfront consisted of little else — heated discussions would have been conducted over mugs of beer, with husky men staging impromptu demonstrations of their preferred tactics, watched by bemused fellow patrons. And on street-corners across the entire United States, money was changing hands at an alarming rate, with the supporters of both Sharkey and Fitzsimmons equally vehement in their loyalty. For working men around the country, the chance to gamble on two of their own in a winner-takes-all test of supremacy was one surely not to be missed.

Naturally, the effervescent Fitzsimmons was never in any doubt about the result, and wasn t backward in saying so, simultaneously delighting the newspaper headline writers and irritating his opponent, who certainly didn t share Bob s impish sense of humour. Behind the Cornishman s usual brand of casually reckless optimism and belligerent boasting, however, was a white-hot desire to dispose of Sharkey as cleanly and efficiently as possible. So it was with a special gusto that he embarked on his traditional pre-fight training programme, setting up camp in the pretty waterside community of Sausalito, a short boat-trip from San Francisco. Today, Sausalito is a favourite stopping-off point for tourists visiting Northern California. With beautiful galleries and craft shops, it s famous as an artists colony and centre of laid-back aesthetic culture — but back in 1896, artistic finesse was in short supply, as Fitz slammed a series of sparring partners around the ring, one after another. Such was his enthusiasm that, as usual, he didn t know when to stop. In all things, the concept of moderation never really seemed to enter Fitzsimmons s head. As a result he suffered a slight hand injury during one particularly frenetic sparring session, which actually caused him to ease off training in the last few days before the contest, much to the concern of his long-suffering trainers. Meanwhile, a twelve-mile daily run kept his stamina at peak level, as exhausted companions struggled to keep pace with the same boxer who d been written off by some as a weakling .

A problem arose, however, which had little to do with either boxer s stamina or strength. It was the question of who would oversee fair play in the ring — a daunting task, by anyone s reckoning. The National Athletic Club, who were promoting the fight, suggested several top referees, but the opposing camps were unable to agree on a final choice. An alternative solution presented itself. The former gunman Wyatt Earp was in town on business. Retired from the rough and tumble of his particular calling, he was now a respected businessman and elder statesman figure. Who better to see that the mere temptation of corruption didn t creep into what was often, after all, a less than virtuous profession? It was felt that Earp was unlikely to be swayed by corrupt promoters, cheating fighters or partisan crowds. After all, a man who d shot and killed at least ten men — including his own brother-in-law—was hardly likely to be cowed by a few catcalls. Discussions with the former deputy revealed that he d overseen several bare-knuckle fights during his early days in the old West, so he wasn t completely oblivious to ring etiquette, such as it was. In terms of his suitability for the job, that was as much convincing as the promoters needed. As usual, Fitzsimmons protested, as he d been warned of some foul play afoot, but again as usual, he was firmly over-ruled.

When Sharkey and Fitzsimmons at last came face to face between the ropes at exactly 10.40 p.m. on the night of 2 December 1896, it was the familiar slightly-built figure with a large handlebar moustache who stood between them. In fact, the start of the bout had to be delayed for several minutes as the ex-marshal paused to remove his frock coat and gun belt, which held a murderous-looking six-barrelled revolver. There was a gasp from the crowd as he handed the weapon to an aide — it was rumoured to be the same 45-Special which had once blazed at the OK Corral.

Their bodies glistening with sweat, both men breathed hard, each holding the other s powerful arms at bay. As the two clinched tightly, Sharkey s bull-like head thudded into the side of Fitzsimmons s face. Booing at such foul play was quickly dispelled by a frown from Earp, who was rushing breathlessly around the ring in pursuit of the two fighters. Despite the physical difference between them, the Cornishman was proving to be his opponent s superior. A succession of ferocious clubbing blows had already consigned Sharkey to the canvas twice; battered and bleeding, he looked like a school bully finally getting his come-uppance. His face was a mixture of astonishment and exhaustion as a rapid-fire series of powerful, accurate punches snapped his head left, right and left again. Each missile aimed from the shoulder was a bomb exploding on the Irishman s jaw, rocking the weight of his body back onto his heels, knocking the fight out of him. It was a familiar story, as Sharkey realised he had met his match — Fitzsimmons was too strong and too quick to be overpowered. Thoughts of a Sharkey victory had already evaporated in the night air — now, it was a question of survival; defending himself against this skilful opponent. Sharkey made a clumsy lunge, in a desperate bid to get out of trouble. But Fitzsimmons had anticipated the move, and was waiting for him. As the Irishman stepped into range, a lightning left-hook knocked him clean off his feet. As he fell backwards, a follow-up punch sent him spinning. He landed on the floor of the ring with an almighty crash, rolling over until he came to rest, face down. The fight was over.

But while the battle had been won, the first shots were about to be fired in an entirely new war. As Fitzsimmons celebrated in his corner, Earp strode over to the unconscious Sharkey and stuffed a $10,000 cheque into his lifeless, gloved hand. The crowd didn t realise what was happening for a few moments, until it was announced that Bob Fitzsimmons was being disqualified for a foul punch, which meant that Sharkey — still slumped on the canvas— was the winner. Immediately, the ring descended into an angry chaos, with both corners arguing furiously over what certainly seemed an unorthodox decision, to say the least. Not for the first time, the moustached ex-marshal was in the firing line; but this time, he couldn t shoot his way out of trouble.

Investigating the latest in a long line of conspiracy theories, an article in *The Ring* magazine, in 1961 sought to explain the events of that fateful night sixty-five years earlier. The original source of this particular theory gave it extra credibility — it had apparently come from none other than Bat Masterson, the ex-lawman who d headed the security detail at the Fitzsimmons-Maher fight in Texas. Black Bat — a long-time friend and colleague of Earp s — had told a journalist a few years after the event that the fight had been fixed. Masterson claimed that Earp told him he d been paid to rig the contest in favour of Sharkey, as part of a secret plan to defraud the bookmakers. Many unanswered questions still surrounded this revelation, such as the fighters involvement. Were they aware of the deal which had been made? Common sense would suggest they weren t, as the punishing pace and physical toll of the fight made a fix seem unlikely. Earp, meanwhile, had vehemently denied any wrong-doing during subsequent investigations and lawsuits. He later told Fitzsimmons he hoped there were no hard feelings between them. At the time of the fight, Fitzsimmons had naturally complained to all who d listen, and many more besides, that he had been robbed , but the referee s decision being final, he was grudgingly forced to accept it.

As surely as night follows day, these two larger-than-life characters, Earp and Fitzsimmons, were destined to meet up once more — and this they did, at the climax of a world-title fight some years later, in which Fitzsimmons had just fought an epic, nerve-draining battle to take the crown. As the ring filled with seconds, well-wishers and newspapermen, the Cornish fighter felt cold steel being pressed to his neck, and glimpsed the heavy barrel of a large revolver being held by his head. Trembling with fear, he turned to look at the man wielding the gun, only to find himself staring into the cold eyes of Wyatt Earp. Amid the hubbub around them, Earp broke the stalemate by draping his other arm around Fitzsimmons s muscular shoulders, laughing. Gesturing at the rowdy crowd who blocked their exit, the former sheriff whispered: Keep quiet, Bob, you re perfectly safe. The first galoot that moves a finger in your direction will be pumped full of lead. Wyatt Earp is your friend. With this gesture of protection, Earp appeared to be trying to make amends for past grievances, offering the hand of friendship to the man he d once cheated in the ring. While Fitz was no doubt mightily relieved to hear that he wasn t about to have his brains blown out by the notorious gunman, it may have taken rather more than a few comforting words to cancel out the memory of the $10,000 he d missed out on. As for the truth about what happened on that night in San Francisco, no-one really knows for sure, as all of those involved have long since taken the secret to their graves.

7. Winner Takes All

As his fame spread, Fitzsimmons continued to enhance his reputation as a people s champion by hazardous means. Namely, by embarking on a new, updated version of his famous travelling roadshows. For some eager young men, the sparring session with a world title holder was an opportunity of chancing their arm in the glamorous, lucrative world of prizefighting; for others, it was simply a chance to prove how game they were, in the presence of such greatness. This wasn t a practice exclusive to Fitzsimmons — the former bare-knuckle champion John L Sullivan was another enthusiastic exponent of the winner-takes-all sideshow. Many other leading fighters of the day also traded on their reputations in much the same way, provided the money was right. Usually staged in theatres, the modern travelling shows were as popular a crowd-puller as the early dirt-ring free-for-alls. It may seem to have been a riskier venture than ever, as a lucky punch from an enthusiastic amateur could injure or — possibly worse still — humiliate the title-holder. These risks were almost certainly outweighed by the financial incentive, however; for people like Fitz, it s likely the lure of good old-fashioned fisticuffs would have been sufficient in itself. From the start of his career, the Cornish fighter simply couldn t resist the promise of an almighty tear-up. His willingness to fight anybody, anywhere, at anytime seemed to indicate what bordered on a death wish. Fight records from the year of 1893 show that on the evening of 5 September, in Chicago, Illinois, Bob Fitzsimmons single-handedly knocked out seven men in nineteen rounds, one after another. The vanquished were all said to be over two hundred pounds, with the largest standing six feet seven inches tall, and weighing in at around two hundred and forty pounds. Names such as Big Bill Collins and Louis The Giant would seem to suggest that they were unlikely to have been shy, retiring types.

Soon after defeating Tom Sharkey, Fitzsimmons embarked on yet another free-for-all tour, this time offering the then princely sum of $20 to any man who could last three two-minute rounds in the ring with him. The tour had actually begun with another sparring partner, with whom the Cornishman had been putting on a theatrical show, but during a delay in the party s railroad journey that particular fighter had been so distracted by the Pennsylvania mountains that he d wandered off to explore them, with the intent of writing poetry about his newly-found inspiration. Far from encouraging the creative aspirations of his employees, Fitz was harshly dismissive of his colleague s poetic bent: He had the habit of forgetting all about the world, everybody in it, and what was going on, while he was writing poetry — or at least that s what he called it, he later said, somewhat ungraciously. The man s disappearance had caused some friction amongst the travelling group, as they were forced to travel on at first, without knowing what had happened to their fellow passenger. The railroad officials refused to wait, even for a poet, so we had to make do without him, Bob remembered. He later added that a telegram was waiting for them in Williamsport, which read: Regret very much having missed the train, but this delightful country gave me an inspiration. Will follow later. Not a bad effort from the aspiring wordsmith, and the terse reply from Fitzsimmons s manager seemed to confirm that the right man had chosen to pursue a career in prose: Don t bother about following. Hope the inspiration is good to eat. Where shall we send your baggage? Literary efforts aside, this meant an open invitation was extended to every man in Williamsport to take on the great Bob Fitzsimmons for a prize of $20. It was an opportunity too good to be true for many a working man, who would have tested his strength against the elements every day of his life, and for whom such a sum would constitute a significant windfall.

Fitz reported that, indeed, there was no shortage of volunteers, noting with apparent surprise just how many men were willing to risk their good health against such an invincible force as he. Williamsport is a nice, quiet, industrious town, but I never before in my life saw so many men who, for a million-to-one chance of earning $20, were ready to take a sound beating, he announced, with typically devil-may-care confidence. Half the audience who turned up to the show seemed to be aspiring boxers, as almost 200 offers were received by the organisers prior to the first fight. It would have been impossible to accommodate all of these without extending their stay, but the visiting party chose some likely contenders, as, one by one, men entered the prize ring to take on the world champion. Fitzsimmons s memories of the fights provides us with a personal commentary: The first man was an unusually shifty amateur, and during the first round, in which I made no effort to inflict any punishment, he stood up and gave me punch for punch. Capturing the atmosphere of tangible excitement present in the hall, he related: At the end of the first round it appeared that the entire contingent of would-be fighters were my opponent s seconds, as the suggestions and advice that poured in from all parts of the theatre were as startling as they were confusing.

One can imagine the pandemonium which would have been caused, as the local lad at first appeared to be trading equal punches with the the great Ruby Robert, conqueror of such characters as Jack Dempsey and Tom Sharkey. Purveyors of local folklore would no doubt have been standing by, ready to anoint the young man as an all-conquering hero, a real-life David who d vanquished a modern-day Goliath. If the fighter — a local miner whose name has long since been lost in the mists of time — was planning to launch his professional career, however, he would have done well to wait until the second round before planning his first world title challenge. He was in for a rude awakening. Our less-than-impartial commentator takes up the story again: The second round started, and I went right after the miner, so as to get him out of the way . . . I landed a right and a left to the jaw, which evidently gave him all he wanted, for instead of getting up, he remained on his hands and knees and crawled off the stage. A less-than-dignified exit from the boxing arena perhaps. But, on reflection, it was probably a wise one.

The next opponent was also a miner, a fact which could immediately be deduced by all, due to the fact that he was covered in grime and was carrying a cap with a lamp on it. In addition, he had obviously brought his own trainer with him, for as the men squared up to fight, a woman s voice screeched from the balcony: If thee don t punch him, Jim, I ll bang thy lugs for thee when thee comes home! Having paused to first decipher and then reflect on this encouraging message, the two approached the centre of the ring. The henpecked Jim didn t take his wife s threats to heart, it seemed, because he hadn t yet succeeded in laying a hand on the Cornishman when a viciously well-aimed punch split his upper lip in two. This bloodshed caused consternation up in the balcony, as the unfortunate man s wife-cum-manager ordered him to stop immediately, before he was seriously hurt. She then turned her ire onto the startled Fitzsimmons, haranguing him for hitting her husband and threatening him with his life if he touched poor Jim again. It says a lot for her combative manner that the man who d outfought some of the most feared prizefighters in America hesitated for a second. He turned to Jim, and asked him if he wished to continue. I had better not , his erstwhile opponent replied, I don t much mind what you do, but it s her I m thinking on. Wise words indeed, from a man accustomed to surrendering gracefully. Although he hadn t thought to bring his wife with him, the third contender of the evening fared little better, seeing stars and crashing to the ground after only one punch. It was there that the boxing challenge ended, as the long list of applicants suddenly dwindled to zero.

The rest of the tour was almost as eventful, as city after city turned out its strongest young men; all of whom would meet the same fate, humbled by a great man. During a stop in Oil City, a local middleweight champion by the name of Harry Coleman caught Fitzsimmons s eye, as he later wrote of a young man who made things very lively — in fact it was as good an exhibition of boxing as anyone would wish to see . The difference between local champion and world-beater was made clear, though, when Coleman tried to step up the pace. He landed a right-hand and a left-hand on Fitzsimmons s jaw, to the delight of the crowd. But when Fitz replied with a solid punch between the challenger s eyes, the force of the blow forced him back on his heels. When the tide seemed to be turning against the promising hopeful, the Cornish veteran shouted across to ask if he d had enough. Not until one of us is counted out, came back the reply, and before many more moments passed, one of them was!

Further along the tour, the town of Scranton had been so excitedly awaiting the Cornish fighter s arrival that they d been conducting try-outs, in order to select the best men for the job of facing him. The cream of the local athletic clubs had been chosen for this most arduous challenge, and it would certainly have been with no little amount of nerves that those men would have watched the infamous old campaigner climb through the ropes. One of these young bucks actually succeeded in drawing blood from the world champion, in itself a significant achievement; after all, to lay gloves on Fitzsimmons was more than many world title challengers could boast of. The man responsible for raising local pride is semi-anonymous, as records only contain his surname — that of Donlin. At the time, he was reputed to have recently beaten a well-known giant boxer named Sandy Ferguson in his home town of Boston. So we can assume he was no stranger to the physical demands of the prize ring. Just as he dealt Fitzsimmons the glancing blow, the older man fired his own warning shot, landing an accurately-placed glove on Donlin s advancing jaw, with his customary blinding force. The two punches landed as one, and both fighters stepped backwards and simultaneously began to bleed from their injuries. For some unknown reason, this co-incidence struck Fitzsimmons as hysterically funny, and he laughed aloud in the ring much to the annoyance of Donlin, who assumed he was poking fun at him personally. Spitting blood from his cut mouth, and muttering darkly about giving him something to laugh at , Donlin laid into his opponent with all the spirit he could muster, taking the fight to Fitzsimmons in revenge for his wounded pride. It must have been quite an impressive display by the local man, as Bob later recorded in his journal that it had been a good, hard slugging round . By the next round, Fitz appeared to have stopped chuckling long enough to remember what he was supposed to be doing, and put his mind to the job in hand. Showcasing the extraordinary ability which had placed him in the highest echelon of the sport, he effortlessly punched Donlin hard enough in the stomach to double him up, and leave him gasping for breath. As the victim was sinking to his knees, the Cornishman delivered the *coup de gr ce*, slewing a stiff shot across his chin, executed with a well-practised ease. This mighty wallop knocked the man backwards with enough force to flip him into a somersault, leaving him resting unconscious and upside down on the sagging ropes, his head resting on the floor, and feet splayed in the air. The curtain went down. Another show was complete.

By anyone s reckoning, Edward Dunkhorst was a giant of a man. Weighing just under twenty-two stone, and standing six foot three inches tall in his bare feet he was, at the best of times, an unprepossessing sight. He was popularly known as the Human Freight Car — for obvious reasons — although history doesn t record whether anyone called him this to his face. Nicknames aside, he was a much-feared professional fighter, who used his massive size to intimidate lesser opponents, many of whom may well have been simply frightened into submission. He was renowned as someone who could punch like the very kick of a mule, putting his considerable weight behind the blows meted out by his ham-like arms, and inflicting heavy damage at close range with his club-like fists. And the rumour was that this man wanted to hurt Fitzsimmons. Badly. So keen was he to carry out this threat that when his nicely worded requests were ignored, presumably because of the champion s busy schedule, the challenges became more and more impatient, until finally they were followed by insults.

Surprisingly, this unorthodox approach seemed to do the trick, as Fitzsimmons s backers arranged a fight between the two at a venue in Brooklyn, which, at that time, had yet to be connected to the main sprawl of what would become New York City. It seemed Dunkhorst s reputation had gone before him, with a clash between the two said to be likely to create a popular attraction. Amid mounting speculation as to their respective merits, the two men — little and large — finally faced each other on 30 April 1900.

WINNER TAKES ALL

Although he doesn t refer to it in his personal recollection of the occasion, it s this bout which is thought to have inspired Fitzsimmons s most famous saying. On being asked if he feared the hulking man mountain, it s said he proclaimed, with a wink: The bigger they are, the harder they fall.

If Dunkhorst himself ever believed Fitzsimmons was genuinely afraid of him, his ego was to be deflated almost immediately. On entering the ring, Fitz took one look at his giant opponent and immediately burst out laughing. It was the sheer size of the man which he apparently found so comical, but Dunkhorst seemed to suffer a severe sense of humour failure at his opponent s irreverent funny bone. That s the last laugh you re ever going to have! the indignant man-mountain bellowed, as the referee sent them to their corners, with Fitzsimmons still giggling like a schoolboy. He would later remark, with biting wit, that Dunkhost was said to be based in the State of Ohio for a very good reason — that no one town or city was big enough to accommodate him. Clearly irritated that the champion obviously wasn t taking the contest sufficiently seriously, Dunkhorst charged out of his corner at the bell, his outsized frame bearing down on the Cornishman like a stampeding bull. He dashed headlong across the ring, his speed belying his vast bulk. But caution should have been advised, as his long-awaited moment of fame was about to pass all too fleetingly. Fitzsimmons swung a crashing punch which caught the huge man square on his jaw, stopping him as if he d been shot and knocking his enormous frame clean off his feet. He crashed over backwards like a building being demolished. The contest was over. Almost as soon as it had begun. The unfortunate Dunkhorst was lying prostrate on the floor, twitching like a beached whale. As his seconds finally brought him round with smelling salts, he asked: Was anyone else killed? His aides, fearing brain damage, asked: When? When the roof fell in. The Human Freight Car had been well and truly derailed!

A similarly unsuccessful — yet far less fortunate — pretender to Fitzsimmons s crown was a man named Con Riordan. The huskily built young boxer squared up to Speckled Bob on the evening of 5 November 1894. The show, which took place in Syracuse, New York, was scheduled as the latest in a series of exhibitions, largely stage-managed affairs, where the men would go through the motions for the benefit of a paying crowd. Neither would get hurt, both would get paid, and the crowd would see a first-class display of ringmanship. Everyone, in theory, would be happy. In theory. That was the script, but on the evening in question, both actors decided to improvise — with disastrous results. The tragic events which would unfold that evening would place a dark cloud over prizefighting in general and Fitzsimmons in particular, almost causing him to quit the sport he loved for good. The root of the tragedy lay with Riordan — a strong, skilful performer, but one who would never scale the dizzy heights of stardom; rather, he would spend his entire career propping up someone else s fight-card, a workman-like journeyman compared to Fitzsimmons s flashy showmanship.

Possibly as a result of the comparatively lowly position in which he found himself, Riordan had taken to seeking his solace in the bottom of a whisky bottle. Ironically, the means of support to which he turned was doing him a great disservice, as his fitness and sharpness began to wane even further as a result. On the night of 5 November, he d drunk more than usual, certainly enough to prevent him defending himself adequately in a prize-ring of this calibre. However, no-one seemed to notice his condition, and he put on the gloves to go three rounds with his boss, as part of the touring show. It was almost certainly the effects of the alcohol, but Riordan chose this particular occasion to show the crowd what he was really made of. In a clear attempt to topple Fitzsimmons onto the canvas, he set about the Cornishman with some hefty jabs and heavy hooks. With a mixture of anger and surprise Fitz realised what his mutinous employee was up to, and the whole nature of the fight changed immediately, as theatrical niceties were cast aside. Oblivious to the crowd and their surroundings, they could have been in a downtown bar or backstreet alleyway, such was the venom and vigour of their efforts from then on. Fighting toe to toe, no holds were barred in this thinly disguised brawl. It was soon obvious why one man was a world-rated champion, and the other a mere foot-soldier. Piston-like fists slammed into Riordan s head and chest, spinning him from side to side and forcing him backwards, like a swordsman on the defensive. Damaging blows rained down on him from all sides and angles. Already unsteady on his feet, he was beaten into submission within minutes, slumping to the floor in a daze, soundly chastised for his audacity and impudence.

As he was carried to the ringside, however, it was soon realised that something was very wrong. He collapsed again shortly after the fight and was rushed to hospital. Two hours after he d been counted out in the ring, Con Riordan died of his injuries in hospital.

The shock of the incident devastated Fitzsimmons in a way that no-one had ever seen before. Despite the protests of his wife Rose, he insisted that the death would mark the end of his fighting career. Never again would he step through the ropes to face an opponent. Matters were made worse when the New York authorities decided that Fitzsimmons must be brought to account for his role in the circumstances surrounding Riordan s death, and he was arrested and charged with manslaughter. One of the all-time low points of his life, it was an abyss from which it would have seemed almost impossible to escape. As well as having the loss of a young life on his conscience, the boxing hero was facing a substantial prison sentence. As so often happens, things gradually came into perspective. Once the initial shock of the death had subsided, calls for the sport to be banned were repeatedly made, along with calls for Fitzsimmons s head. These calls may seem familiar to modern-day boxing enthusiasts. But they soon gave way to those of greater reason, and the manslaughter charge was summarily dropped soon afterwards, when the inquest jury decided that Riordan had been in no condition to fight, and had contributed to his own misadventure.

If anything, the public reaction was one of sympathy for Bob, whom they felt had been treated like a scapegoat by authorities clean to wash their hands of prizefighting for good. The whole episode affected Fitz more than was widely known at the time and it was some while before he could be persuaded to once more take up his chosen calling, without the fear of history repeating itself. He told his wife that he was frightened of what his bare hands were capable of, now that he d seen the permanent damage they could unwittingly cause. For a man possessed of such awesome power, Fitzsimmons was clearly also possessed of a rather more sensitive disposition than many gave him credit for. And while he went on to win ever greater honours in the sport which adopted him as its own, it s unlikely he ever forgot the name of Con Riordan; a man whom the same sport had harshly rejected.

9. Physical Fitness ... and 'Gentleman Jim'

The extent of physical injuries inflicted by two fit, strong men engaged in all-out combat can easily be imagined as bone and flesh collide with sickening force. It s somewhat harder to estimate the reserves of steel will and courage, coupled with sheer resilience, which have to be heavily drawn upon when one s body comes under such ferocious assault. Fitzsimmons often spoke of his distaste for bare-knuckle sport, having been appalled by the condition in which his early opponents had been left. Towards the end of his career, this attitude also seems to have applied to the art of boxing as a whole, as his appetite for conflict began to leave him. It was during this time that he famously remarked that he would only attend a boxing match if his services were called upon by a friend to act as a second.

During his prime, he and his colleagues were forced to endure the most terrible abuse imaginable: bones were broken, faces cut to pieces and heads pounded senseless in ordeals which sometimes lasted up to six or seven hours. Nowadays, it s perhaps more difficult to understand exactly what would spur a man to merely stay on his feet, when he has suffered the equivalent of a serious road accident. Among today s ringside doctors, limited rounds and strict supervision, there is less room for punishment; so when a fighter is seriously injured, he can be swiftly treated and removed to hospital at once. Back at the turn of the century, enduring the repeated agonies of the ring was not only requested by trainers and audiences, it was demanded.

On one particular occasion, Fitzsimmons entered into a fight having suffered a suspected broken arm in training the day before.

The arm was bound tightly with a tube to drain the infection from the limb, and he gamely carried on, despite the obvious pain he was in. He later admitted that the reason behind this was purely financial — quite simply, he desperately needed the cash. In the years prior to that ordeal, he was also subjected to smashed knuckles, torn ears and gashed eyebrows, sustained over many years in the sport. Often he ended a fight barely able to stand, having sustained the most appalling injuries: his face battered beyond recognition. During his early career, he regularly feared for his day job, as broken hands would render him unable to work as a blacksmith. As his career progressed, conditioning therefore became paramount, as only those in the prime of fitness could hope to even confront the rigours of a top-class competition. Above all others, Fitzsimmons was a living example of this finely-tuned training and preparation. A magnificent physical specimen, his body was honed to muscular perfection, with scarcely an ounce of fat to be found on his lean frame. He attributed the colossal strength of his powerful chest and shoulders to the many hours spent labouring at the anvil. And although those days were now far behind him, nevertheless, hammering out horse-shoes remained a vital part of his pre-fight training. One writer described him as being built like a human fighting machine . He said:

> Bob Fitzsimmons is built like a boy from the feet to the waistline, and then he becomes a triangle. He has the most powerfully wonderful shoulders one could find in a city of a million. His shoulders are so tremendous that his head looks much smaller than it is, for it is a perfectly normal head with grey matter in its walls that thinks so quickly that in a battle he has thought and acted before his opponent has had time to think about fighting.

As the boxer advanced in age, he claimed his industrious training routines, coupled with a healthy diet, meant that he remained in tip-top shape. He once boasted: I am credited with throwing to the wind the pet theories of trainers, doctors and athletes, through my knowledge of the body of the man I am fighting, as well as the method of my training. I have always done my best to preserve the body and health given to me, and have always studiously avoided abusing it in any way. He continued: I do not drink any alcoholic beverages. I do not use tobacco in any form. Those two things alone are as beneficial to a fighter as any amount of athletic training . . . the burning of the candle at both ends is the death of the athlete. A man cannot overeat and drink, and remain in a fit condition. This message seemed to be borne out by his legendary fitness, which would see trainers and companions flag and collapse by his side during his lengthy runs. A typical day during training would see Fitz rise at four o clock in the morning and embark on a twelve-mile road run. On his return, he would go for a swim and then be rubbed down, before breakfasting at 8 a.m. He would then rest until 2 p.m., when he would start an exhibition of sparring and bag-punching. A favourite training location was that of Skagg s Springs, near San Francisco, where he had a purpose-built platform in front of his hotel, so people could watch him work. His diet was always strictly controlled, in order to maintain his fighting weight. He explained: What you eat, what you drink, and when you eat and drink have a lot to do with your health, and spell either defeat or victory. There is nothing in the world that will prolong life in man, woman or child as will the quiet home existence and regular hours of the average Englishman. Fine words indeed, but as Fitzsimmons s fame and wealth grew in later life, rumours began that he wasn t always true to his pledge of abstinence. If he wasn t burning the candle at both ends, he was certainly singeing it slightly in the middle.

But this was still some way off. For the time being, he was undergoing the most punishing regime of his life, with each work-out, run or exercise aimed at fine-tuning his physical performance, during the ultimate endurance test ahead. For the long-promised fight with his nemesis, the heavyweight champion James Corbett, he trained as he d never trained before, attacking his usual training runs with even greater enthusiasm than before. He would say in later years that this was the most important bout of his life. I d have gone into the ring with Corbett if there hadn t been a dollar in it for me anywhere in sight, and I think he knew it just as well as I did. His managers probably wouldn t have cared to hear such scandalous talk, but it shows the depth of feeling behind Fitzsimmons s preparations. I put the time in, for I knew that if I was going to whip Jim, I d have to be there when the final gong tapped.

While Fitz regularly wrestled with lions and bears as part of his unorthodox fitness campaigns, the comparatively harmless pursuit of swimming was strictly off-limits. This followed a colourful episode some years earlier, when a member of the animal kingdom almost put paid to his career forever. As he tells the story, he was training in New Orleans for a forthcoming fight when he fell victim to a mosquito attack while relaxing in his bed. He rushed out of bed and tore his clothes off, running out of his lodgings to jump from a nearby pier into a river, in order to rid himself of the biting insects. As he launched himself into the water, he spotted two enormous alligators circling below. Thrashing the water to a foam, he escaped with seconds to spare, as the two huge reptiles pursued him to the bank. He gained revenge the next night, using a 45-calibre revolver to shoot two large gators at the same spot. If I didn t kill those two I certainly killed two others, which was just as satisfactory to me, he later claimed, adding that the narrow escape had changed his training methods forever. I cut out swimming from that time on, except in the ocean, where I knew I d be safe from such creatures.

But there were other, rather less exotic dangers on the horizon. These would not be found in the world of nature, but in the roped confines of a boxing ring.

The two men advanced on each other, outraged. Barely-controlled fury was on the point of igniting into full-blown violence; the air crackled with the tension between them. Shaking with anger, they raised their voices in a mixture of taunts and epithets. It was a display of male bravado, a response to a physical challenge; the avenging of an intolerable insult. Dressed in sports clothes, the men were lean, muscular and exuded physical danger. In either of their company, a lesser man would have backed down without hesitation. But neither was a lesser man. Nor did they have any intention of backing down. With just a few feet between them, two sets of powerful fists were clenched as the situation threatened to spiral further out of control. Quickly, other men on the scene stepped in between the two, restraining them with difficulty before any harm could be done. The raucous shouting and bawling continued; stabs of harsh noise in the quiet air. This was no ordinary confrontation. The two men were not street thugs and the scenario wasn t being played out on the backstreets of a tough city. They were highly paid athletes, in the last stages of training for their forthcoming match. The two combatants had come within a hair s breadth of an unseemly street brawl, narrowly avoiding the indignity of an unceremonious and highly-publicised scuffle. Each was easily capable of killing a man with his bare hands — a fact proved by their reputations as two of the most successful and highly-paid prizefighters in the world. Their names were James Corbett and Robert Fitzsimmons.

The match that the entire sporting world was urging to take place had at last moved a step closer to becoming reality. Since their last meeting, when the initial contract had been drawn up, a good deal of legal parrying had been played out. To say the meeting would be a rather tense affair was an understatement akin to stating that the Grand Canyon is rather wide or that Corbett found Fitzsimmons rather irritating. The two, dressed in fine, richly tailored clothes, had glared fiercely at each other throughout the early negotiations at a New York hotel — a face-to-face meeting which had been set up to carve out a deal which was satisfactory to all. The pressure on the fighters representatives to please their employers would have been heightened by the fear that the two fighters were likely to start a private bare-knuckle bout then and there, in the event of one false move. It was at this stage that Fitzsimmons repeated his claim that he would fight Corbett for free, for the sake of giving the confident Irishman a damn good beating; while Corbett, in turn, let it be known that he was only agreeing to meet Fitzsimmons on extreme sufferance, clearly believing the Cornishman to be his sporting and social inferior.

This verbal parrying signalled that the first punches in the mounting war of attrition between Fitzsimmons and Corbett would be fought with business agents, lawyers and counter-bids, rather than the one-on-one battle which had been promised to the public. In the days of ever-increasing prizes for crowd-pulling fighters, it was a scenario which was becoming almost as familiar as the actual contests themselves. Perversely, it actually served to heighten the anticipation, as the sniping and back-biting helped the process to gather momentum. Like the unfortunate fracas on the training run, this bartering market was itself simply a form of macho posturing. Each fighter had his price for sure, but it was up to his manager and entourage to push this price as high as possible. Champions, they said, don t come cheap.

A delicate balance had to be achieved; each slice of the metaphorical cake had to be carefully measured. Each fighter had to feel that he was being properly rewarded for risking his life in the ring. Even more importantly than this, they had to be reassured that their reputation was such that they were being paid at least as much — and preferably more — than their opponent. Petty squabbling, akin to that of jealous siblings, actually lay at the root of all the pre-fight discussions, all the contract negotiations and the hard-nosed hustling. But while fighters were indeed a marketable commodity, the final judgement would ultimately rest with the paying public; they would fix the price, both in terms of audience sizes and perceived value for money.

In the case of Corbett and Fitzsimmons, an added ingredient had already spiced up these proceedings considerably, no doubt much to the satisfaction of their respective press agents. It had become startlingly obvious that the two men genuinely disliked each other. Since their earlier scuffles, they had been carrying on an increasingly bitter feud, with each blaming the other for the antagonism. The sports pages of New York newspapers at the time would often carry quotes from Corbett describing Fitzsimmons as an upstart Englishman who d been too big for his boots for far too long. Similarly, Fitzsimmons would publicly accuse Corbett — in even more colourful terms — of running scared, refusing to fight him. It was the sort of name-calling which may well have seemed more at home in the school yard, but beneath the quotable prose there may have been several reasons for the deep-seated antipathy. Firstly, although his father was Irish, Fitzsimmons was generally seen as an Englishman, which was a major handicap to start with, as far as his all-American counterpart was concerned. Fitzsimmons also came from a very different school of experience, with his working-class background and street-fighting spirit. The reasons which made them such an attractive billing — the relatively cultured, middle-class bank worker, pitted against the rough-hewn, immigrant blacksmith — also reinforced the divide between them. Also, it must be said, the Cornishman had been blessed with an uncanny ability to rub people up the wrong way, which, in part, was due to his child-like over-exuberance. Corbett was far more reserved in both demeanour and outlook, and it was clear the two were never going to see eye-to-eye on the current politics of their chosen profession, much less anything else.

Of course, the public loved it. The rash of ever more insulting newspaper headlines dutifully served to whip up a growing wave of enthusiasm for boxing into a huge tide of popular support. It would just make the moment when the two finally clashed all the more dramatic. This contest had already gone far beyond a mere fight. For both men, this was a personal mission. When the fateful day finally arrived, it seemed as if the entire United States of America was excitedly awaiting the outcome. After all the bragging and taunting, both in person and in print, the two most popular fighters in the Western world were finally going to meet up in anger. Corbett had already emerged as the favourite. As the defending champion, he was expected to out-box and out-manoeuvre the gangly Cornishman, using his famous scientific tactics to wear down the opponent. Fitzsimmons, on the other hand, was seen as an outside bet, as students of form knew he was more than capable of stopping the American, if he caught him off-guard with one of his legendary punches. As if testing these animal instincts, he found relaxation between his heavy training schedules by wrestling with Nero, his pet lion. This caused high amusement among onlookers, and equally high concern among his backers, who may have foreseen their expensive investment being mauled to death before their eyes. For Corbett, of course, there was no such frivolity in his training regime. He applied what he called the science of boxing to prepare his game plan, focusing on Bob s perceived weaknesses to map out how he would take the fight to him, and knock him out of contention.

The town chosen to host this celebration of prizefighting was one famed for its trailblazing heroes. Carson City, in the state of Nevada, took its name from the pioneer Christopher Kit Carson, who discovered the territory in 1843-44, along with the explorer John C Fremont. Carson City was a typical old-time Western frontier town, with an action-packed history. It was established as a community in 1858, the first trading post having been set up there some seven years previously. When President Abraham Lincoln declared Nevada a state in 1864, largely due to the importance of its gold and silver deposits to the Union s Civil War effort, it was Carson City which claimed the accolade of being named capital. The honour was bestowed at the constitutional convention at the time, and it remains to this day. The discovery of gold and silver on the Comstock Lode in the 1850s led to Carson City s emergence as a major centre of trade. Mines in Virginia City, Gold Hill and Silver City provided ore for local mills, while wood for mine timbers was brought from the Sierra Nevada mountains. The city was home to the United States Mint from 1869, a site which is occupied today by the Nevada State Museum. Throughout the 19th century, Carson City gradually developed into one of Nevada s principal communities. It is those facts that must have given significant weight to its bid to stage the big fight.

So it was that on 17 March 1897, at a sports arena located at Musser and Harbin Streets, thousands of fans queued several times round the block in order to witness what promised to be one of the greatest sporting occasions of all time. The streets were swamped with a never-ending tide of people, pushing and shoving to cram into the arena. The air would have been thick with tension and excitement as those lucky enough to get in rushed to ringside. Today, this historic site is occupied by the Carson River Basin but back then, it witnessed a crowded, noisy amphitheatre, crackling with the pure emotion of a gladiatorial gala. A rule was enforced that all men should give up their weapons before entering. The arsenal which piled up by the entrance would have supplied a small army; more than three hundred in total. A man who was himself no stranger to firearms, the infamous Wyatt Earp, watched from his position in the crowd, possibly remembering the last time he had come across Fitzsimmons and the controversy which followed. The ring in the centre of the huge crowd was the focus of all attention, as the thronging crowd waited anxiously for the two men to leave their dressing rooms. Finally, it was about to happen — James Corbett from San Francisco, would take on Robert Fitzsimmons from Cornwall, in order to decide who would be the heavyweight champion of the world.

In getting this far, the two fighters were already breaking new ground; and, once again, it was not without some considerable controversy. The Nevada Legislature had legalised prizefighting only a few months before, and the bout had come under heavy criticism from public figures and press from neighbouring states. Promoter Dan Stuart stated his intention that it should be a good, clean fight; neither brutal nor crooked. (In later years, the contest would be seen as a watershed, as other states began to look again at their strict anti-prizefighting laws, and began to stage fights of their own — no doubt with the financial rewards from the Corbett v. Fitzsimmons fight firmly in mind. In turn, the sport began to adopt a more civilised, open image — a significant step away from the backstreets and dustbowls where it was first conceived.)

The fight would also make history for an altogether different reason, besides its sporting significance. It would be one of the first fights to be recorded on film; this technological development had only been made possible a few years previously. The result would later be shown to cinema audiences across the country, who were said to be astounded by both the picture and its contents. Many people had led sufficiently sheltered lives as to never have witnessed a boxing match; so as well as providing a cultural education, it further heightened the profile of the once-reviled sport.

Mindful of previous ructions over refereeing, the highly-charged task of ensuring law and order between the ropes was put into the safe hands of George Siler, who d begun officiating when gloved boxing was first introduced, and had conducted the short-lived bout between Fitzsimmons and Peter Maher. Famed for his integrity and honesty, the barrel-chested, moustached Siler was an excellent choice, combining a detailed knowledge of boxing with a strong sense of fair play. He may not have brought six-guns into the ring in the style of his colourful predecessor, but his stern expression showed he was clearly a man who would brook no foul play. He actually doubled up as referee and fight reporter, later filing a report of the night s action to the *Chicago Tribune* for whom he was employed as a senior correspondent. Modesty meant that his official verdict of his own performance was, unsurprisingly, left to others to judge.

Miraculously, the film survived, and can still be viewed today. For those who ve followed the exploits of Fitzsimmons and his contemporaries, it is a bizarre sensation to actually watch the man in action, so many years after his death. The flickering, grainy image focuses on the sun-bleached ring, as seconds in hats and top-coats finally prepare the two fighters for battle. Then, as the moment of boxing history at last draws near, the combatants approach each other: Corbett, dark-haired and well-muscled, Fitzsimmons, freckled and bald. Despite the passing of time, the sheer force present in that Carson City prize-ring can still be sensed. The action on screen is at first halting, often untidy, as the men scuffle, push and pull, but the power of the blows reminds the viewer that this was truly not a sport for the faint-hearted, whether they be a participant or a spectator.

As the pair climbed through the ropes to thunderous applause, Fitzsimmons appeared unconcerned by the hubbub which must have almost deafened him. Wearing bright-green gloves and dressed in his robe, the former blacksmith paced around the ring, gazing out over the sea of faces which seemed to stretch to infinity. He d always denied suffering from stage-fright, claiming to be able to concentrate his attentions on the matter in hand. This reverie was broken, however, when one particular spectator, sitting by ringside, said within his earshot: Corbett ll knock his head off. Look at what he calls legs! Notoriously touchy about his slender lower limbs, and no doubt further on edge amid the atmosphere, Fitzsimmons angrily shouted down at him, You lack the artistic temperament. My legs are all right!

Continuing his walk around the ring, he paced slowly, head down, as if deep in reflective thought. He waited for Jim Corbett to enter the arena and he could have been forgiven for feeling very alone — an Englishman in a foreign land about to take on a man who was a national institution, before a huge crowd of rabid fans. It says much for his constitution that he was able to appear so calm, amid such a cauldron of pressure and anticipation. He later described his feelings as the cheers and general cacophony washed over his lowered head, as the world waited for the show to begin. He reflected: How did I feel then? I ll tell you. Did you ever go out with a gun after something big in the game line? Do you remember how you walked about, waiting for a chance? Just one look at what you d come for? Remember the jump that went through you when you caught sight of it? That s it; that s just the way I felt when Corbett turned around and faced me. As the preliminaries got under way the scene was more akin to a dress parade than a prize fight. The pomp and circumstance was yet another indicator of just how society had embraced an activity which had previously been considered sufficiently unpalatable to warrant criminal prosecution against those who took part in it. Compare this scene, for instance, to that of the Texas Rangers being unleashed to stop the Maher fight in Langtry.

One noticeable social nicety was missing from this stage of the proceedings however — that of the traditional Englishman s handshake. This was usually intended to show that the physical conflict which would follow was purely in the interests of sporting competition, rather than a personal grudge. We can assume that this contest belonged to the latter category, as Corbett adamantly refused the gesture. I will shake hands with Fitzsimmons when he has whipped me, he announced. The events that followed would serve to remind everyone of the reserves into which a fighter has to dig if he is to overcome a deadly opponent. Every nerve was tested to breaking point, then tested some more, as the two men put on one of the most breathtaking displays of man-to-man combat. As the hot Nevada sky burned above them, the massive crowd roared their appreciation, goading and spurring both men to further acts of bravery.

A leading sports writer of the time, Thomas T Williams, was at the ringside, and later said that it was one of the most magnificent showcases of physical combat he d ever seen. He wrote in his report of the fight that he d expected Corbett to have the best of the contest from the start, with Fitzsimmons s only chance of victory resting on his explosive punch hitting the target, and stopping the contest there and then.

The heat was stifling; each corner takes great care to vigorously fan its man down with towels while anonymous, long-forgotten men with large cowboy hats look on nearby. The difference between the two is apparent — Corbett the stronger, but Fitzsimmons more game, taking lashing blows to the head, while returning a heavy hail of punches about his opponent s torso. The Cornishman appears to favour a laid-back stance, almost as if he s leaning back on his haunches, inviting Corbett to enter the danger zone. The American seems ready to chase his quarry, and it s he who enjoys the best of the early rounds, battering Fitzsimmons s bald head left and right with a steady, grim determination. Ruby Robert suffered heavy facial injuries in the early rounds, with only his fitness and spirit keeping him in the fight. There are times, when the two tangle, that Fitzsimmons s lack of physical size becomes clear, but the speed and range of his punches rock Corbett back onto his heels. The flickering, unsteady film shows two men battling in glorious monochrome.

Commentators weren t prepared for the savagery of the broadsides which rained down on both boxers, nor for the extent of the injuries they inflicted. The majority of the crowd appeared to be supporting Corbett; unsurprisingly, since an Irish-American could count on the emotions of a native crowd on St Patrick s Day. But there were awed into a near hush by the courage of the challenger, who braved everything the champion could throw at him, and still replied with full-blooded attacks of his own. Corbett was every inch the dashing blade, his dark hair falling across his forehead as he punched, dodged and parried. But Fitzsimmons, his face a mask of concentration, was lashing out with venomous force, while blood became smeared with sweat across his speckled features. Corbett s finely tuned skills caught the Cornishman at every opportunity, with the latter s head whipping around under the force of the American s mighty forearms. Not long into the fight, Fitzsimmons had suffered a torn lip, a bloody nose and swollen ears. His eyes heavily bruised and half-closed, he fought by instinct; blinking with pain at the bright sunlight. This was the fight when Fitzsimmons really showed what he was made of. The joking and the boasting were forgotten.

Our ringside correspondent Mr Williams, a seasoned fight observer, found himself captivated by Fitzsimmons s visage, battered yet unbowed. He wrote: I saw the face that will haunt me until time has effaced it from my memory. It was a mixture of pathos and tragedy. There was no savagery in it, but some intelligence. There was a leer and a grin, and a look of patient suffering and dogged courage. It was the look of a brave man fighting an uphill fight . . . you cannot compare it with anything, for there is not another human countenance like Fitzsimmons s when he is fighting against odds. The haunted look which could be seen on the Cornishman s face, as he tangled again with the awesome Corbett, was reflected on that of his wife at the ringside. Rose Fitzsimmons s delicate features winced at every shuddering punch that crunched into her husband s body, and blinked in hope when a powerful right-hook smashed into Corbett s head. Blood from Fitz s face coated Corbett s gloves, while the champion s muscular body was also spattered with crimson, as the former blacksmith continued to soak up punishment. But while things seemed to be going very much the Californian s way, he just couldn t deliver the knock-out that the crowd so keenly anticipated. Each time he tried to finish the task, his opponent s head ducked down between his shoulders, before skipping out of trouble. In fact, the Cornish fighter s lasting endurance was worrying Corbett s corner, who were looking more concerned as each round went by. Where Fitzsimmons s corner had reached the depths of despondency in the opening rounds, with his trainer looking close to tears, now they sensed that sheer durability seemed to be matching Corbett s ringwork. It was, quite simply a war of attrition. At one point, the bout seemed to be over, when a particularly vicious cross from Corbett slammed into Fitzsimmons s nose, causing blood to spurt across the canvas floor. Fitz sank to his knees, his face grotesquely distorted by the effects of the champion s fist. But somehow, he found the strength to rise unsteadily to his feet, and gamely launch another combination towards Corbett s weaving head. The scornful laughter which had been seen in Gentleman Jim s corner fell abruptly silent. There was a very real fear among the seconds that the man who seemed to have all but lost the fight was actually getting stronger, recharging his energy beneath the matted mess of blood.

In the eleventh round, it was a worried man who faced Fitzsimmons. Corbett s wind had all but gone, sapped by his own energetic style. And now he seemed more and more in peril, as Fitz showed no inclination to back off. A particularly frenetic spell saw Corbett pushed into a corner and dealt several blows about the face which saw him lolling from side to side. This time it was his face that began to take on a battered look, as the blacksmith s notorious punching power doubled him up with pain and, with gathering momentum, rocked him back on his heels. He rallied with some fearsome swings of his own, and both men defied their fatigue to stand toe-to-toe, trading terrible body-blows. It was a sequence which would be described by one observer as the hardest and fastest fighting he d ever witnessed. The many calls of Game boy, Fitzsimmons which now fell on the ring told their own story. The crowd was turning. They d seen a man travel to hell and back, and they began to sense victory in his continuing determination. Corbett, becoming increasingly desperate, swung at Fitz s jaw but missed, with the momentum throwing his own body off balance. The moment which decided the result occurred in the fourteenth round, and it was a sight which one seasoned observer commented that he never wished to see again. Guerilla warfare had once more quickened into all-out attack and the Cornishman now had the American at his mercy. Finally, a blow from Fitzsimmons hit Corbett so hard in the midriff that his fist appeared to drive into his stomach. A follow-up blow to the face knocked the breathless champ out of the fight, as it was immediately clear that the burly boxer wouldn t be doing anything for the time being, much less defending himself. Having sunk to his knees, he grabbed at the ropes for support, with his eyes upturned so that only the whites were visible. His face was deathly white, as he grimly fought for breath. The referee counted him out.

Robert Fitzsimmons was the new heavyweight champion of the world.

The film of the fight captures that precise moment. Boxing history caught on celluloid for all to remember. Fitzsimmons s lethal and momentous punch to Corbett s midsection will live on forever. The punch is said to have landed with excruciating power on the spot of his solar plexus. From the pictures, this can t be confirmed as the speed of the incident blurs into a brief flurry of punches, but Corbett can clearly be seen slumping to the floor. With Fitzsimmons s fearsome anvil-trained upper-body strength, the effects of such a strike can only be imagined as excruciating. America s home-grown hero of the canvas had been knocked from his throne by the irrepressible Englishman. As the camera continues to roll, Corbett crouches in agony, Fitzsimmons raises his arms aloft and referee George Siler steps between them with an air of finality which signals the end of Corbett s reign. Ruby Fitz , the fighting blacksmith , had just become one of the most famous men in the world. Back in London, the thousands of people thronging the streets for news of the fight would later hear that their man had knocked out the famous Gentleman Jim Corbett to become world heavyweight champion. In New York, around fifty thousand people had gathered in City Hall Park, waiting to hear the first news from Carson City. Joy mingled with dismay when word came of the Cornishman s astonishing victory, for the fight had divided the country in its loyalty. Back in London, the mood was one of sheer, patriotic pride. It had been England against America and England, in the form of a thirty-five-year-old man from Cornwall, had won the day.

The bald-headed brawler had captured the sport s ultimate accolade and it would catapult him to a stardom which would change his life forever. Fame, fortune, riches, all were now within his grasp, and never was a man more keen to reach out and grab them. No-one present at that infamous bout could have realised the significance of the night s events. It would be one hundred and two years before a British-born man achieved the same feat, ensuring the name of Robert Fitzsimmons would loom large in the halls of fame for a very, very long time to come. The Cornishman later re-lived the moment which would change his life forever. He said: I feinted with my left hand, swung the right to miss, going over

Corbett s head, and brought my left to his stomach, constituting the famous shift; and then without changing my position at all, landed the same left to his jaw as he was sinking. That is how the championship was won by me. One sportswriter said that the look on Fitzsimmons s face in the immediate aftermath revealed a cunning, streetwise fighter who d carried out a pre-determined plan of action. I saw that he knew what he was doing. The moment he landed, his face told the story of a successful general s coup, he wrote.

While the upset would cause chaos throughout the sporting world over the coming days and weeks, chaos had already taken root in that Nevada prize-ring when George Siler finished his count. Corbett s corner protested, claiming that their man had been felled with a foul punch, but the experienced referee waved away their protests, insisting the move had been fair and legal. Crowds of people from the audience began climbing into the ring, in defiance of police instructions, both to congratulate Fitzsimmons and commiserate with Corbett. Corbett himself took the news badly, to say the least. As soon as he d recovered himself, he launched himself at the Cornishman, seemingly ready to fight all over again, albeit outside the Rules. The two men were quickly separated, with Corbett swinging wildly at anyone who got in his way, while shouting at the man who d beaten him. As the riotous m l e continued, Fitzsimmons s corner showered adulation on their man — the man who was now the best in the world.

10. The New World Heavyweight Champion

Virtually overnight, it seemed that America had wholeheartedly embraced its new heavyweight champion as a worthy successor to the sport s top trophy. In doing this, they lost no time in transferring their affections from Corbett, which would in itself have inflicted an extra blow on the fallen idol. True to form, the conquered gladiator was far from magnanimous in defeat, claiming that Fitzsimmons had merely succeeded in landing a lucky punch. I was off my guard and don t know how it occurred, he complained, while nursing his injuries. All I feel is pain near the heart. I shall challenge Fitz at once to another fight to the finish. I am defeated without a scratch. I was not knocked out, but counted out through being winded. The depth of his humiliation was evident in his parting statement. I would rather have been killed, he moaned.

While Corbett was putting a defiant face on his loss, stubbornly repeating his claim that his opponent had merely winded him, a report of the former champion s medical condition immediately after the fight tells the full story. It said that he had suffered a great shock to his nerves, with an examination showing that his blood circulation was weak. He suffered bouts of vomiting immediately after the contest, while also experiencing severe aches and sore muscles. The report said that the boxer was treated with doses of morphine to help him cope with the pain. Not that the glory-chasing world of boxing gave much thought to Corbett s ailments. It was far more concerned with ceremoniously crowning the new king of the big men . Indeed, newspapers of the time actually claimed that the public had scant sympathy for the ex-title holder, because of his arrogant bragging prior to the fight. The $20,000 loser s purse may have eased his suffering somewhat, but it s likely a good part of this would have had to be immediately paid to his father, who had confidently — and somewhat rashly — bet his entire life savings and the family s livery business on his son successfully retaining the title. All things considered, that dusty day in Carson City had been something of a disaster for the Corbetts.

As for the Cornishman, well, he could certainly have been forgiven for withdrawing from the public eye for a while after the celebrated duel. This would have given him time to reflect on what had been a magnificent victory, while also licking his wounds and generally taking stock of the life which was no longer his alone. This was, to a certain extent, exactly what he did. He wasn t to don the gloves for another two years. Some observers feared that he had no intention of stepping into a ring ever again, such was the sudden gap he left in the boxing scene. For better or worse, the fight world was certainly a far duller place without him. His absence attracted strong criticism from some areas of the press, who accused him of protecting his title by running scared from likely contenders. A cartoon appeared in one particular newspaper cruelly depicting an extremely unflattering caricature of Fitz, complete with freckles and bald head, being bodily dragged into a boxing-ring by rivals such as Corbett and Maher. It s likely the old English—American rivalry was partly to blame for this rather hostile feeling, as the host country was no doubt keen to reclaim the title which it had dominated until now. In any case, it was hardly unusual for a fighter to rest on his laurels in such a way, whether he was motivated by money, prestige or caution.

One theory was that the Cornishman was taking his revenge on Gentleman Jim for keeping him waiting during the run-up to their title clash. This seemed to be supported by the fact that negotiations for a re-match repeatedly stalled, and finally disintegrated altogether, with Corbett eventually abandoning all attempts to lure the new champ back into the ring. In truth, the real reason for Fitzsimmons s continued absence from the ring was due to an entirely different calling. It was the smell of the greasepaint which was temporarily diverting Fitz s attentions from his day job , as he enthusiastically pursued theatrical ambitions. Cynics claimed he was milking his status as the new heavyweight champion by accepting lucrative engagements in theatres across the country, while clearly ignoring his pugilistic obligations. Of course, there may have been more than a grain of truth in this charge, as Bob s finances were perpetually in need of replenishing, thanks to his poor business sense. His financial advisers may also have had something to say on the subject, as his management is thought to have received up to fifty per cent of his earnings, from wherever they originated. Equally likely, however, was Fitz s personal yearning for stage stardom which opened up this particular career option. After all, he was not usually a man to accept any kind of advice or instruction. A thespian role would fulfil his desire to entertain people, without the nightly occupational hazard of being punched half to death by a man twice his size. He d flirted with the concept of treading the boards for some time, juggling occasional vaudeville appearances with his more traditional public performances.

His first wife, Alice, had harboured ambitions in this direction since their early days in Australia, and now Rose s influence, along with that of her brother, would almost certainly have fanned the flames still further. It was popularly believed to be Rose who played a significant role in keeping Bob out of the ring, as she d publicly announced after the trip to Nevada that her husband intended to retire from boxing, thus bowing out of the brutal world which had almost crippled him. It can t have been easy to watch her beloved husband fighting for his life before a roaring crowd. The sight of his blood-spattered face in Carson City was one which would have stayed with her. She was, therefore, happy to back him in his other showbusiness pursuits, even combining business with pleasure by regularly appearing with him on stage.

Unfortunately for Fitzsimmons s new career, these contrasting alter-egos appeared to cause something of a problem in the minds of the theatrical profession. Certainly a degree of typecasting restricted his thespian roles somewhat. He was usually cast as a boxer, a blacksmith, or both, and there seemed to be a lack of other roles to suit his specific talents. His performances as a boxer were said to be highly convincing, as one would expect, although fellow actors required to spar with him as part of the story often suffered as a result of the boundless energy he brought to the part. A significant part of the attraction for the audience was having the opportunity to see the world heavyweight champion at such close quarters in such unusual circumstances.

Initially, theatre-goers may have been alarmed to find out that these roles often required the leading man to flex his vocal cords in song, but it seems any possible fears were largely unfounded. To give the fledgling performer his due, the quality of his singing voice was surprisingly good, while the sight of the muscular ex-blacksmith hammering away energetically at an anvil while heartily belting out a chorus would have truly been a sight to behold. Reports describe him possessing a reasonable tenor voice. Obviously emboldened by this, Bob s voice also often featured as part of the night s entertainment in many a high-spirited celebration or general drinking spree. One of his first professional appearances was in a play named *A Man s A Man*, which he followed up with a series of variety shows involving boxing exhibitions, lectures and discussions. These roughly took the form of a one-man show in which he demonstrated, talked, answered questions and talked some more.

He also appeared with his wife in a play called *The Honest Blacksmith* in which he fought with the villain of the piece, much to the likely dismay of that unfortunate actor. Bob s popularity was such that his acting performances were extremely well-received, even if there were unlikely to be any artistic awards in the offing from the profession he had so recently entered. His natural good humour and instinctive sense of comic timing immeasurably (and often unintentionally) livened up many a performance. In contrast with his early career, audiences were often reduced to gales of laughter at his efforts.

In fact, a later production actually proved to be something of a box-office success. The melodrama *The Fight For Love* enjoyed well-received tours, while also achieving the improbable feat of casting Fitz as the romantic hero. Publicity photos of the time show the rugged prizefighter elegantly attired in an immaculate white suit, obviously enjoying the role of the lovelorn heart-throb. With his rapidly thinning hair parted almost over his left ear, he cuts an unlikely Romeo figure, but audiences continued to warm to the man who had so often assumed the role of real-life hero.

After the birth of their daughter Rosalie in 1899, Rose Fitzsimmons retired from the footlights to concentrate on their family and home life in New York. She is said to have thrown herself entirely into this calling, effectively turning her back on the acrobatic career which she had once enjoyed with her brother. This is possibly also due to the fact that Martin Julian s own days were now taken up with keeping the world heavyweight champion under control, or at least trying his best to do so. The siblings were united in this effort, for Rose s own responsibilities took over where her brother s left off. At best, Fitz was likely to get under her feet in their Bath Beach home; at worst, he could be a downright nuisance. Clearly, he needed to keep his mind occupied, and rather like a child, when he became bored, he got into trouble. While at home, he did his best to keep out of mischief by hammering out a lengthy route on strenuous daily runs. He also liked to pursue the sports of wrestling and hand-ball in the grounds of his house, while still maintaining a steady workload of training at his gym.

Gilbert Odd wrote that during one such comparatively tranquil period, the fighter decided to make his own entertainment and personally arranged a showcase bout at Madison Square Garden with a talented English middleweight, Geoff Thorne. Thorne was a promising talent, although he d recently been stopped by the famous Kid McCoy in New York. Fitzsimmons took considerable time and trouble over the arrangements for the bout, which he prepared with the help of Thorne, due to the fact that the two Englishmen had become firm friends. Skulduggery was clearly in the air, as Fitz took great care to personally train Thorne for the fight. Although this oddity — a fighter preparing his forthcoming opponent — could be explained by the fact that it was purely an exhibition bout, to be staged in aid of charity, the two boxers spent many hours working on their techniques. It seemed as if the old campaigner was handing down a few hard-learnt tips to the younger man.

PRIZE FIGHTER

The Cornishman s reputation ensured a good turn-out for the event and a good number of fight fans were present to see the pair square up in the ring. All was proceeding without incident, when a right-handed blow from Thorne suddenly landed flush on Fitzsimmons s chin. The veteran immediately crashed to the canvas. Looking rather bewildered, Fitz just managed to beat the count, scrambling to his feet and groggily raising his hands once more. The tempo of the competition had been raised a few notches and the crowd gave their full support by urging the protagonists on. After dodging Thorne s flailing fists for some time, Fitzsimmons responded with a shuddering left hook, which knocked the young man clean off his feet. In turn, Thorne climbed back up from the floor, and ran at Fitz, swinging his right fist into his opponent s unguarded face, and knocking him down again. The crowd were unable to believe what they were witnessing, as Bob got up again and faced Thorne. He swung his left fist round, which sent the Londoner sprawling yet again. Once more, Thorne climbed to his feet. Exhausted, they circled slowly, both men seemingly on the point of collapse. As one, they threw mighty punches, which connected with their targets simultaneously. The two fighters both collapsed onto the canvas, where they lay still, one on top of the other.

A bemused referee counted both of them out, and when this count was complete, both Thorne and Fitzsimmons sprang to their feet and embraced, laughing uproariously. The spectators, having realised they d been completely duped by the well-choreographed fake, cheered all the louder. The two actors took their bows, and strutted back to the dressing rooms, arm-in-arm. Clearly Fitzsimmons s sense of theatre had once more come to the fore.

If anyone was left in any doubt about the true merits of each boxer, these were answered several months later, when they met for real in Chicago. This time, the theatricals were left in the dressing-room, as the only dramatic moment came after less than a minute, when Fitzsimmons knocked the young man unconscious with a vicious left hook.

11. The Prodigal Son Returns

It wasn t until he d truly established himself as one of America s top sportsmen that Bob Fitzsimmons finally returned to the land of his birth. The prodigal son who d captured the imagination of the British public as a larger-than-life action hero, doing battle in a foreign field, was at last coming home. For the first time since his family sailed across the world in search of a new beginning, Robert Fitzsimmons made the pilgrimage back to the country where it all began. The people who d idolised the champion and cheered on his exploits from afar were no doubt anxious to welcome back their illustrious countryman and reaffirm him as one of their own. The boat that took him away from his birthplace would have borne a bright-eyed young boy, in turn both excited and scared, possibly dressed in the hand-me-downs of his elder brothers. Twenty-four years later, when the luxury liner SS *Trave* coasted into the port of Southampton, it carried aboard it a worldly man of supreme confidence and great authority, wearing the finest clothes money could buy, and surrounded by a showbiz-style entourage. As a world boxing champion, Fitzsimmons was a schoolboy s fantasy come true; a man who d achieved an impossible dream with a style which made you believe he was born for it. Everywhere he went, he was f ted as a conquering hero. Flashbulbs popped and waiting crowds cheered. Fans turned out in huge numbers to see the dapper gentleman with top hat and walking cane carry out a series of public engagements. Like a movie star, they called his name. This man, who d come from obscurity, was taking his place among the sporting superstars of the new century.

His first engagement was as a guest of the London boxing community with several of its members taking their hero to see the

Derby horse race. Fitzsimmons would have been well at home among the great and the good of the sporting world who regularly attended such occasions. The day s entertainments were completed by a top-class dinner at the Palace Cafe in The Strand. The celebrated ex-patriate was also invited as a guest of honour to the Olympic Boxing Club in Birmingham, where he was presented with a gold-topped cane by its adoring members. He did put on the gloves during his visit, but only for show, sparring briefly with a man named Anthony Diamond, to the delight of those who d come to witness the formal occasion.

It s not known whether he actually visited those members of his family who had remained in Cornwall; or even if he travelled down to his birthplace, but the reception from the public at large proved that Britain had taken him very much to her heart, confirming his status as a true Englishman. The feeling was mutual — the boxer constantly referred to Helston as his home, and often talked of early memories from his childhood. Due to the politics of the boxing business in America, Fitzsimmons been forced to adopt US citizenship in order to compete for world championships, but it was a move he d undertaken with the greatest reluctance and regret.

Fitzsimmons s next recorded visit to his homeland wasn t for another thirteen years, when he would make the voyage with his third wife, Julia May Gifford. The pair were taking their stage play on an international tour, as Bob s ring career was nearing its end.

There are conflicting reports as to whether he actually put on the gloves himself during this stay, but one record shows him meeting the English heavyweight William Iron Hague. Boxing historians have since said this was likely to have been a non-competitive exhibition bout. The Cornishman would certainly have put on a sufficiently entertaining display for all the Britons who d so far been denied seeing him perform in the flesh, and with precious little time to do so, before he hung up his gloves for good.

But this was all to come in the future. Back in 1899, there was the matter of defending his world heavyweight title, after his lengthy layoff. Another fight. Another opponent.

12. Back in the Ring

Coney Island, New York
9 June 1899

Their tired faces cut and swollen, the weary, bloodstained warriors paused to gasp for air, drawing on their last reserves in order to continue the slow torture. Steam rose from their sweating bodies, while their fists remained clenched and their torsos taut with tension. The two men had reached an impasse and both were suffering heavy usage, but neither was willing to back down and accept defeat. For his part, James Jeffries, the man challenging Bob Fitzsimmons for the world heavyweight championship, looked like a man who d just been hit by a tram. His left eyebrow was torn open, with a flap of skin protruding over his eye. A deep gash on his cheek had smeared his entire face deep crimson. The effects of Fitzsimmons s crashing fists pounding relentlessly on his head and body would be with him for some time to come. Referee George Siler, who d separated the two from a clumsy, exhausted clinch, now waved them together once more. With heavy limbs, they once again began circling each other, each consciously wary of the other s inherent danger. Jeffries body was suddenly jolted, as if by a severe electric shock. He d been hit by a succession of hammer-like swings, which jarred into his midriff with the force of several steamhammers. Fitzsimmons had earned a reputation as possessing one of the most deadly punches in boxing, and the full extent of his punishment could be seen on the younger man s pained expression, although he remained resolutely upright in the face of the constant barrage. In turn, the Californian used his muscular build to power several shots into the side of Fitzsimmons s head, catching him around the ears and on the side of the jaw. Even for someone of Fitz s resilience, the flashes of white-hot pain must have been excruciating. Shrugging off the hurt, he ducked nimbly away from more of Jeffries searing blows.

Each came back at the other with renewed gusto, and each gritted his teeth as knuckle, once again, connected with flesh. To the delight of the crowd, the two mighty heavyweights were putting on one hell of a show.

A swinging left hand smashed into Fitzsimmons s face with a force, sending a tremor through his lean frame. As he swayed, another glove slammed into him like a train. He rocked backwards, but somehow remained on his feet, weightless and fighting for balance. This was lost for good with the occasion of yet another explosive punch from Jeffries, which contained all the might generated by the young man s fearsome physique. This last direct hit was the one that finally sent the Cornishman sprawling to the floor, where he crashed into an ungainly heap. At thirty-eight years of age, Fitzsimmons was finally beaten; by a twenty-six-year-old prizefighter who d proven himself to be the better man. The duel had been long, brutal and bloody. It left a sufficient impression on Fitz that he recalled the experience years later, describing its dying moments: I was falling around with my hands at my sides, both my eyes closed, absolutely dead to the world. I am told that Jeffries met me from a crouching position with his right, and landed right on my left eye tooth. Down I went, and I was counted out. I had lost the championship. I was utterly unable to realise what was taking place. It seemed that Fitzsimmons s rich seam of form had finally run out. His apparent invincibility in a prize-ring throughout so many contests and against so many opponents, had been lost, at the precise moment his body slumped to the floor at Jeffries feet. It was Jeffries who was now the undisputed heavyweight champion of the world, and with Fitzsimmons nearing forty, it seemed unlikely that he d scale that particular summit again. He d fought like a tiger, enduring the fiercest punches that the younger man could throw, and hurting the ambitious challenger with numerous shots of his own, but no-one could argue with the result.

No-one, that is, apart from Fitzsimmons himself. Once more, it seemed controversy was about to rear its head, as he claimed there was a reason for his defeat, one which defied either ability or condition. He caused one of the biggest sporting furores of the day when he went on to claim: I know it is not a very nice thing to cry after you have been defeated, and I don t think it s in my make-up, after my long ring career, to wail at an honest defeat, because I know quite well that every man at some time meets his superior in every walk of life. He went on: I claim that during that fight, I was drugged. My physical condition was such and my ring generalship so far superior to that of my opponent, that it was only by drugging me that it was possible to take from me the Heavyweight Championship of the World.

The extraordinary allegation consisted of a theory that his mineral water had been tampered with during the fight, which left him weary and sleepy. He had no actual evidence to back his theory, but a newspaper reviewer of the time said in his report of the bout that Fitzsimmons appeared to be dazed , adding that when he came out for the fourth round, he did not appear at all like himself . Fitz later said that prior to this round, his manager and brother-in-law, Martin Julian, was forced to actually push him back out into the ring, just as police officers overseeing the fight began to take an interest in his condition. I wanted to lie down and go to sleep when Julian said Stand up, Bob, the police are going to stop the fight , and I am told that I did stand up and that the police, seeing me, thought it was all right, and so did not interfere.

He took pains to point out that he didn t blame Jeffries personally for the alleged tampering, as the two were actually good friends. I don t for one moment say, or even believe, that Jeffries took any part in the drugging, if drugging there was, or that he knew anything about it. Jim and I are the best of friends; we have spent a great deal of time together, we understand one another, and I would not even think that Jim Jeffries would permit such a thing to happen in any fight in which he was interested, either as principal or in any other capacity.

Fitzsimmons insisted that his suspicions had been aroused because of another strange happening which had preceded the fight. He d been training in the gym which he d built at his home in New York, and had gone out for a run on the boulevard near Coney Island. On his return, his manager told him that Jeffries manager had stopped by and had asked that the fight be postponed for two weeks because his fighter wasn t fully fit. As Fitzsimmons had been sparring and working out with the set date in mind, he was less than pleased at this development, proclaiming that Jeffries condition was no concern of his, and that there was no leeway in the rules for rearranging fights in this manner. But Fitzsimmons s manager had already agreed to the deferred date, so Bob had little choice but to go along with it. He would later cite this as a further example of the alleged one-upmanship within the Jeffries camp. But nothing was ever proved and no further action taken. Jeffries was judged to be the rightful winner of the contest, and was therefore heralded as the new world heavyweight champion. But Fitzsimmons would continue to claim, to anyone who d listen, that foul play had robbed him of what was rightfully his, all the while insisting that he was the better fighter.

Reports of the fight don t back up Fitzsimmons s claims, for there is no other mention of his being drowsy or in any way impaired, although it could be argued that such symptoms would be difficult to spot among the all-encompassing fatigue of such a bruising encounter. One newspaper report described the dying seconds of the fight, as Jeffries moved in for the kill: Jeffries advanced carefully. Then his long left crashed to the jaw of the champion. A feint at the body was followed by a powerful left again to Fitzsimmons s jaw. His knees buckled, and his brain was benumbed. It went on:

> Jeffries launched his right with 205 pounds behind the toss and it landed with a thud against Freckled Bob s jaw. He fell. Jeffries stood and looked down on his defeated opponent while referee George Siler counted the doleful decimal. Fitzsimmons lay on his back. His eyes were closed. His blood-stained shoulders quivered. The great arms that had wrenched up the crown from Corbett, doubled up the powerful Tom Sharkey and hammered Gus Ruhlin into submission, lay inert at his side. Over him swept the cheers that he had so often heard before, but this time they were not for him. They were for a new fistic hero from the Golden West.

These were not words that Fitzsimmons would ever have wanted to hear, but in between his accusations of foul play, after the shock had sunk in, he did actually find time to pay Jeffries the respect that he deserved. During one of his rather more reflective moments, Fitzsimmons privately admitted to his wife Rose that regardless of what may or may not have happened behind the scenes, Jeffries had simply been too big and strong for a man of his age to contend with. He described Jeffries punching as the most powerful he d encountered, and reflected that every time he d landed a punch on the Californian, one had come back, twice as hard. Rose herself would say in public that her husband hadn t been in the right condition to fight, and she claimed that the defeat was due to this reason. Personally, however, she may well have felt differently. She d wept bitterly when her husband finally collapsed at Jeffries feet — his first stoppage on American soil. The fiercely loyal wife and mother was said to have been particularly affected by witnessing the beating, and she was said to have been still in tears when the Fitzsimmons entourage returned to the house at Bath Beach. Cut and bruised, Fitz was taken to rest in the bedroom, where his wife immediately joined him, sitting on the bed and comforting the fallen hero as best she could.

The Jeffries fight was also a traumatic one for Martin Julian, marking a distinct cooling in the relationship with his brother-in-law and client. Theirs had always been a distinctly uneasy partnership, partly due to the fact that Julian was now married to Alice, Fitz s first wife, and bringing up Charles, Bob s son, as his own. The other factor which constantly caused friction, however, was the fact that Julian seemed to have little or no influence in the boxing world, often being seen as a hindrance to his charge s career. The former acrobat did possess a renowned talent for putting his foot in it, and this ability was always going to be a dangerous element around the volatile Fitzsimmons, who certainly didn t count diplomacy among his finer points.

A prime example of their pulling in different directions occurred immediately after the Jeffries fight, when the manager announced to reporters that his brother-in-law was unbowed by the defeat, and would immediately fight to re-stake his claim for the title as soon as possible. Fitzsimmons himself, on the other hand, no doubt having been given a talking-to by Rose, told journalists the following day that he had no intention of ever setting foot in a ring again. When this apparent contradiction was pointed out to him, he was highly embarrassed, declaring that he would speak to Julian about the matter and put him straight. This he did, in typically understated style. A full-on screaming match ensued when the manager eventually turned up at Bath Beach, with Fitz — rather bizarrely — accusing Martin of betting on Jeffries. He also berated the hapless businessman over the alleged drugging, repeating his claim that something had been placed in his mineral water, and demanding to know if he agreed with this theory. Martin shouted back that it was the effects of Jeffries fists that had put Bob to sleep, rather than the water. With Fitz s wounded pride still smarting, this observation would have been welcomed rather like a bull welcomes a red rag. Having said his piece, Martin stamped off in a huff, while Fitzsimmons raged interminably at this shocking display of disloyalty. It seemed he d found a convenient release for the frustration which had undoubtedly built up since the loss of his title. A newspaper report in the *Mirror of Life* newspaper gives a blow-by-blow account of another bust-up between the two during this stormy period — this time at the Lyric Theatre, New York. An innocuous mix-up over free tickets (Martin was one of the managers of the theatre) led to an angry exchange, in which the manager — rather foolishly, to say the least — actually struck the boxer. The recently-deposed world heavyweight champion replied with a punch which immediately opened up a cut on Julian s face, before they could be prised apart. This marked the death knell of their colourful relationship. If they hadn t been separated, it might also have marked the death knell of Julian himself.

The recent defeat represented an altogether new experience for Bob, and it was clearly one which was anathema to his fiercely competitive nature. Age was an ever-present factor, as he entered his thirty-seventh year, but Fitzsimmons passionately believed in his own ability, remaining absolutely convinced that he possessed the vital ingredient of a successful world-class boxer. There were some grounds on which to make this claim; although he may have slowed slightly in his speed around the ring, and his reflexes may have softened a mere shade, the sum total of his experience and durability under fire would have at least partly compensated for this adjustment in style. No doubt desperate to prove he was still a big box-office draw, he agreed to take on one of the latest challengers for Jeffries new crown, a man named Gus Ruhlin from Ohio. Ruhlin had notched up an impressive win over Tom Sharkey, inflicting such a fearful beating on the former seaman that the referee was forced to intervene before the end of the fifteenth round — an unusual measure in the early days of prizefighting. Sharkey s roughly hewn features had been transformed into a bloody mess by the sheer ferocity of the abuse they d suffered.

There was precious little opposition for Fitzsimmons elsewhere at the time, as Jeffries had just defended his title successfully against the persistent James Corbett, who was also keen to claw his way back to the top of the pile, so the paths of Fitzsimmons and Ruhlin were scheduled to cross on 10 August 1900. The timing was crucial, because changes in the already-strict boxing regulations were about to restrict the audiences of such fights, so promoters were busily feathering their sporting nests while they still could. Records of the fight recount how, shortly after ten o clock that evening, referee Charlie White drew the two men together and they shook hands, before coming out of their corners primed and ready for battle. Ruhlin — nine years Fitz s junior — immediately proved he was no pushover, stabbing the Cornishman s face with a series of stiff left jabs, opening up a cut over the older man s left eyebrow and drawing blood from his mouth. Ruhlin was using his considerable weight advantage to good effect — he was almost six feet two inches tall, weighing just under fourteen stones — and he stopped the action at the death of the first round, bringing Fitzsimmons to his knees with a particularly cruel blow.

Where Ruhlin made a mistake, however, was not capitalising on his advantage immediately. Possibly without realising it, he eased up slightly in order to conserve energy, and this allowed his game opponent to claw his way back into the fight. Fitz had been around a long time, and he d fought many battles. Renowned as a wily streetfighter, it was a foolish man who underestimated him — even for a second. All the same, a niggling hand injury, sustained in a previous fight, was beginning to cause him trouble. It was neither the first nor the last time that Bob s battered knuckles would conspire against him, making him a victim of his own powerful punching. As the bout went on, Fitzsimmons drew level with Ruhlin, and the two were soon matching each other punch for punch, as fans from both sides crowed their excited approval. Bob s darting fists were starting to catch his opponent and Ruhlin soon began to bleed heavily from a cut mouth. A right hand to the jaw and a stunning left which thudded into his body made the man from Ohio stagger and reel back towards the ropes. Fitz seemed to have his man beat, as Ruhlin stumbled and fell forward onto all fours, but the bell interrupted the count. Events evened out again in the ensuing rounds, as fatigue began to set in on aching arms and heavy legs. Both men were bleeding profusely from facial wounds, with blood spattering across the ring, as blow after blow continued to land. It was not a place for the faint-hearted, and of the two protagonists, it was Fitzsimmons who seemed to be resisting tiredness rather better, using his ring tactics to spoil, block and clinch. A flurry of swings at Ruhlin s head brought him down again, with blood pouring into his eye from another fresh cut. Urged on by an anxious Jim Corbett at the ringside, Ruhlin staggered to his feet and tried to shake off the effects of the attack, but he was looking more and more like the loser of this fight. In the next round, Fitzsimmons rounded on his opponent. Tenaciously slashing through the air with his gloves and connecting hard with Ruhlin s head and body, he forced him helplessly back into a corner. It was only a matter of time now, as a shuddering right hand buckled Ruhlin s legs, while a two-punch combination finally sent the young man tumbling to the canvas.

Amazingly, however, he managed to climb back to his feet again and, to his credit, pitched towards Fitzsimmons with the intention of trying to make a fight of it once more. With blood in his sight this time, the former world champion unleashed a frantic series of punches, the last of which was a breath-taking uppercut which lifted his victim clean off his feet, before he crashed down onto the floor of the ring. This time he stayed there. Motionless. While the audience screamed their approval of the keenly fought contest, those fans who d come to follow the Cornishman added an extra vigour to the cheers, no doubt relieved that their man hadn t lost his touch after all. It had been a magnificent performance. His strength and determination had ensured his survival, while his streetfighting instincts had allowed him to ruthlessly plan and execute his attack. Ruhlin remained on the floor of the ring for some time before he was eventually lifted by his corner helpers and carried to his dressing room. His injuries were such that he was disfigured for some time after the fight, unable to join in a planned re-enactment for the movie cameras a few days later. As the breathless Fitzsimmons climbed from the ring, newsmen crowded around him in search of a headline-grabbing quote. True to form, he didn t disappoint. I guess I am still young enough to make things hum for some people , he boasted, in answer to recent speculation over his advancing years. With the bit between his teeth, he continued: I don t like talking in this strain, but I must speak my mind after all the criticism that has been heaped upon me since I lost the championship. Now I plan to get my revenge over Sharkey [referring to the Wyatt Earp incident] and pave the way for a return fight with Jeffries.

The sting in this tale, however, was still to come. Anxious to prove he was as fit as the next challenger, Fitzsimmons claimed he would meet Tom Sharkey in a full-on bout within two weeks, leaving him only days to recover from his injuries. Even for someone who prided themselves on their fitness, this would surely represent a tall order.

Once again, Fighting Bob was in full cry. His freckled, bald head glowed with perspiration as he hurled punch after punch into the muscular body of Sharkey, causing the recipient to gasp, recoil and retreat. Three times, Sharkey swung mighty lunges at Fitzsimmons s bobbing form, and three times he missed. As the two came together, they jostled fiercely, before they could be separated, with Sharkey landing a wild left in Bob s face. A swift follow-up saw Fitz drop to the canvas, but his dazed fall was cut short by the bell for the end of the round. Shaken, but desperately trying to put on a brave face, Fitzsimmons shrugged aside the concerns of his seconds. I m going to sink the ship! he bragged, referring to the three-masted tattoo which adorned Sailor Tom s chest. This was obviously the time for old scores to be settled, and the pace of the fighting reflected the pride at stake. Sharkey tried to capitalise on his attack, but instead walked into a hammer-like thrust from Fitzsimmons which cannoned into his midriff and caused him to slump forward, lolling breathlessly onto his opponent s chest. Having been parted once again by the referee, they both went on the attack simultaneously, with flailing fists again finding their targets. A beautifully-timed Fitzsimmons right hook caught Sharkey flush on the jaw, dropping him to his haunches. When the Sailor had regained himself, further punching from Fitz sent him sprawling onto the ropes, where he vainly tried to escape his opponent s onslaught. Another powerful right hook sent him to the floor again, from where he only narrowly beat the count, returning groggily to his feet.

Sensing his prey was severely weakened, Fitzsimmons launched a lightning-fast flurry of punches from all directions, pummelling Sharkey s head relentlessly. Just as the American seemed on the point of collapse, a fearsome left hook from Fitzsimmons sent him spinning out of control across the ring. He eventually collapsed on his hands and knees, with blood flowing from his mouth. He hung his head in dejection, as the referee finally counted him out.

Fitzsimmons had destroyed two opponents in two weeks, proving he still had what it took to be a world champion. Now there was only one man left to beat — his former conqueror, Jim Jeffries.

13. The Re-Match

Jim Jeffries was a force to be reckoned with. The pretender who d challenged and taken the Cornishman s heavyweight crown had always presented a formidable image to the world. A large, barrel-chested man who looked as though he d be more than capable of looking after himself, he had the goods to back up the packaging, and it was a brave man who d tangle with him. He d beaten a number of top-class opponents in bruising style, before finally knocking out Fitzsimmons to take the world title. If there was a boxer of the early generation who filled the role of the stage villain, Jeffries was surely it. The former boiler-maker had a reputation for possessing a mean temper, coupled with a surly, gruff attitude. His publicity photos show his granite-like features filled with dark foreboding. He was kept at arm s length by other boxers, who spoke of his uncompromising nature.

Described by boxing historians as one of the greatest pugilists of modern times, Jeffries was born in Carroll, Ohio, on 15 April 1875, making him twelve years Fitzsimmons s junior. He was said to have come from a family which could trace its ancestry back to Normandy, France. His parents moved to California in 1881, and it s there that the young boy grew up into a hulking giant of a man; standing six feet two inches tall and weighing in at around 220 pounds by the age of sixteen. He was both fast and fit — capable of completing the hundred-metre dash in around eleven seconds. He s described as looking like a big grizzly bear when in action, with next to no style or skill to speak of. Instead, he possessed an awesome, ox-like strength which would simply batter down any resistance offered by an opponent. It was during his job as an iron worker that he learned to box, quickly gaining a local fame which saw him selected as one of Gentleman Jim Corbett s sparring partners. Nicknamed the Iron Man of the Roped Square, Jeffries developed a technique of crouching down to avoid punishment, lacking as he did the speed or agility to avoid oncoming blows. Its a testament to his tough durability that he was able to overcome this flaw to triumph in some of the most bloody ring battles ever seen.

The return match with Bob Fitzsimmons was likely to be just as much of an all-out war as the original meeting, with the Cornishman promising to exorcise the memory of his defeat, while re-capturing the coveted champion status. The match was scheduled to take place in the city of San Francisco, on 25 July 1902. Since they last did battle, Fitzsimmons had resumed his routine of systematically demolishing opponents in quick succession. Still insistent that he d been drugged during the last Jeffries fight, he promised to be in peak shape for this title clash, in order to recover what he considered was his by right. His impressive return to form gave credibility to his oft-repeated claims that the Jeffries fight had been a mere blip in his ascending career path. Before the return match could take place, however, fate would once again conspire to complicate the life of Bob Fitzsimmons, with no little help from the man himself.

Having trained for around five weeks at the gym in his home in New York, he travelled to the summer resort of Skagg s Springs, a preferred location for the agonising schedule of training which he regularly endured, in order to fine-tune his body. In his camp on this occasion were George Dawson, an instructor from the Chicago Athletic Club, Jack Stelsener and an enormous black boxer named Hank Griffin. Griffin was described by Fitzsimmons as a fighter who rated among the best in the country. The logic behind his inclusion in the Skagg s Springs camp may have been to test Fitz to his very limits, to sharpen his honed fighting skills to an extra-fine point.

A typical training routine of this particular campaign would see the Cornishman pound a twelve-mile run in the early hours of the morning, before taking an energetic swim. In the afternoon, he would step into a specially-built exhibition ring in front of his hotel, where fans and sight-seers would be treated to an exhausting display of fast-and-furious sparring and bag-punching. Under the high glare of the Californian sun, each sparring partner would endure six rounds with his highly-demanding employer, where no quarter was likely to have been given, by the super-fit Englishman. Those lucky enough to witness these workouts would have been left in no doubt as to the veteran s determination to recover his title. As a reward for this hard work, occasional trips for the fighters and trainers were organised as a distraction from the punishing routine; these usually took the form of a deer hunt, riding mules up into the mountains surrounding San Francisco.

The sparring sessions became quite a tourist attraction, with the town s mayor and captains of local industry, such as the millionaires John D. Spreckels and Adolf Spreckels, bagging seats by the makeshift ring. It would be these gruelling spectacles which would threaten to undermine the carefully laid plans of the Fitzsimmons corner, notably one particular session with Hank Griffin.

Griffin and Fitz were trading blows, the bigger man having already been urged by his boss to fight for all you are worth . In answer to one of his attacks, Bob unleashed a left hook at Griffin s head, which missed the big man s jaw and jarred awkwardly against the top of his skull. The result of this over-exuberance was that Fitzsimmons s left hand was virtually useless from that moment, quickly swelling to a large, painful stump. Once again, the Cornishman s trainers held their heads in their hands. One stupid mistake, caused by careless over-confidence, was now threatening to wreck his chances of ever reclaiming the championship. Undeterred, Speckled Bob climbed through the ropes on the afternoon of 25 July, crackling with confidence. He was determined to quickly dispose of the young Californian, even without the use of his injured hand. As well as prestige, there was a veritable treasure trove to fight for. Of a sixty-five per cent share of the gate receipts, the winner would receive sixty per cent and the loser, forty per cent. The dollar signs were flashing in the eyes of both corners, as the large hall was packed to capacity, with enthusiastic fight fans from across the country anxiously waiting to see these two go forth into battle once more.

After only a few minutes, history was already in the process of repeating itself. The frantic fury with which both men set about each other threatened to unsettle even the sternest of boxing spectators. Jeffries had already suffered such cruel punching from the older man that it was all he could do to stay upright. It says a lot of his upper-body strength that that he was able to continue defending himself under such a vicious onslaught. Both of Jeffries eyes were bruised and puffy, a large gash had split his forehead, his right eyebrow had been torn open, while his left eye was also badly cut. His nose had been broken in two places under the pounding of Fitzsimmons s fists, and blood was spattered across the whole of his face and chest. The crowd must have been in a deafening state of near hysteria, as the vicious scrap raged to and fro, lurching from one side of the ring to another, like a ship in a storm. Trying desperately to ride the blitz which had been unleashed on him, Jeffries skirted deftly around the danger zone of Fitzsimmons s most vicious punching, trying to avoid the threatened final punch. Swinging wide blows which missed their target, he charged into the Cornishman, butting him hard in his stomach in an attempt to entangle those thrashing arms. In the heat of the pitched battle, shouting at Jeffries to stand up and fight like a man , the former blacksmith smashed his good hand repeatedly into the young man s face again and again, opening up new streams of blood, which again cascaded over his battered features. The crowd noise reached new levels of emotion, as they sensed that the end was in sight. Jeffries only hope was to hold on until the older man began to tire. He was unaware of the challenger s hand injury, but it seemed to have made little difference so far, in the unholy bloodbath of the opening round. Just before the bell sounded, the American was still grimly clinging fast, pinning the hands which had done him so much damage to his opponent s sides. Again, Fitzsimmons bellowed above the ear-splitting noise of the crowd: Let go, Jeff! Let go! I won t hit you in the clinch! It was a small, incongruous nod to the rules of the fight game, in the context of such a terrible mauling.

As the fighters faced each other for the start of the second round,

THE RE-MATCH

Jeffries looked like a casualty of a war zone. As he got to his feet, he swayed slightly and blinked hard. His ear was bleeding heavily, hinting at internal damage. Both his eyebrows were cut open now, and his nose was a mashed, bleeding pulp. His lips were swollen and tortured. Nonetheless, he glared defiantly at his torturer, as they slowly closed in once more. But unbeknown to The Boilermaker, his opponent was also in trouble. Ironically, the tremendous power of his own blows had sent shooting pains up the length of Fitzsimmons s damaged arm, which was now virtually unusable. He went into the round as a one-armed fighter. As the bout settled into a rather less frenetic pace, Jeffries continued to absorb the impact of his opponent s strength. It may have dawned on him that Fitzsimmons was carrying an injury, as any use of the Cornishman s left hand was immediately followed by a sharp gasp. As time went on, it seemed the worst of the ordeal was over for Jeffries, who was now gradually re-establishing himself in the fight. Several times he trapped Fitz in a corner, swinging energetically at the flailing bald head which ducked and weaved in front of him. Beads of sweat darted, as the two men traded blows at close range, each cancelling out the worst of the other s punching. The referee was called on to break up a number of clinches, as Jeffries used this tactic to deflect and delay. Seeming to have gained a second wind, he pursued the old campaigner from one side of the ring to another, but Fitzsimmons was always quick enough to duck under the oncoming gloves. Observers by this time noted that his face had the appearance of a slaughterhouse , with the bone protruding from various cuts over his eyes, while the eyes themselves were swollen to puffy slits. Nowadays, the fight would have been stopped long before a man reached this condition, with medical facilities at the ringside being immediately rushed into action. But back in the rough-and-tumble world of the turn-of-the-century prizefight, it was only when a man went down, and stayed down, that he was judged to have been beaten. It seemed as if Jeffries corner had feared this wouldn t be long coming, as they d been whispering anxiously among themselves, casting worried looks at their man s disfigured face, and encouraging him as best they could during the worst of the beating he d received. Fitzsimmons himself wasn t unaware of the other man s plight. He later said: Jeffries was the worst-looking object that was ever in the prize ring, he was cut up so terribly. I said to myself, Poor fellow, he is terribly punished. It is only the matter of another round before both his eyes will be closed. Then I will appeal to the referee. I cannot hit a man with both his eyes closed, and I will ask the referee to stop it.

As if detecting this sympathy, Jeffries gestured to Fitzsimmons in the ring, putting both his hands in the air, and holding his head on one side. The gesture seemed to be that of a wounded animal waiting to be put out of its misery. To undertake this mercy, Fitzsimmons swung a huge punch at Jeffries head. However, the intended victim deftly stepped aside, and rather than lying down, swung the most powerful blow he d yet delivered, up into the Cornishman s solar plexus. The force took Fitzsimmons s breath away and actually lifted him off the ground. He crashed back down to earth, writhing in agony. Above his pole-axed form, the referee counted to ten. Uproar ensued across the arena, as the Cornishman was finally counted out. He d lost the re-match, and the chance to regain his title, in a manner totally at odds with the one-sided fight. To make matters worse, he d lost it because of the very punch he himself had pioneered.

Accounts of the fight pay tribute to the courage of both men, for putting on such a display of raw aggression and energy. The injuries sustained by both proved just how demanding on body and spirit the battle had been. Both fighters emerged from the two-bout epic with reputations enhanced, as they were now seen as true blood-and-guts fighters, who would fight almost to the death, giving any crowd value for their blood-money. Jeffries went on to become one of the most feared of the modern heavyweights. He eventually retired in 1904, refereeing the match which would anoint his successor as world heavyweight champion. Marvin Hart and Jack Root fought twelve rounds under Jeffries watchful eye before Hart knocked out his opponent to claim the title. Six years later, however, the boiler-maker was persuaded to come out of retirement by his friend Jack London, who was among those leading the hunt for the Great White Hope — a white boxer to beat the black fighter Jack Johnson. Johnson s marriage to a Caucasian woman had turned bigoted public opinion violently against him, leading to a flow of racial abuse and ill-treatment.

Jeffries, several years past his shelf life and seriously out of condition, nevertheless donned the gloves against the Galveston Giant in the town of Reno, Nevada, on 4 July 1910. The contest was promoted by the legendary Tex Rickard, who also acted as referee. In hindsight, it was the worst mistake Jeffries would ever make. The thirty-five-year-old veteran was easy prey for the mighty Johnson, who battered him into a bleeding, exhausted wreck before the fight was stopped by Jeffries corner in the fifteenth round. If Johnson was fighting to defend his race, he did an awesome job.

In the crowd that day were two other characters central to our story, James Corbett and John Sullivan. Corbett, smartly-suited and bowler-hatted, was acting as one of Jeffries advisers , while Sullivan, also cutting a dashing figure in a checked sportsman s cap, was at the ringside to file the story to a Boston newspaper. It was only a few years before that the two urbane gentleman chatting quietly in the front-row seats were tearing each other apart within those very ropes. As for Jeffries, he went once more into retirement, which he spent in his adopted state of California. It was in his home at Burbank that he died, almost fifty years later, on 3 March 1953.

14. Death . . . and Marriage

It was on 17 April 1903 that Robert Fitzsimmons received the most painful blow of his life; its impact far greater than the total sum of all the physical punishment he d ever received in the ring. It was the day when the flame which had ignited his success flickered and finally went out. Rose Fitzsimmons, beloved wife, devoted mother and motivating force behind her husband s greatest glories, died from typhoid pneumonia.

Bob had been taking part in a touring exhibition of boxing with his erstwhile opponent and longstanding friend, Jim Jeffries. The men who d twice all but killed each other in the ring had since formed a close relationship, based on a strong mutual respect. They were visiting towns and cities across the United States, once more giving young hopefuls the opportunity to don the gloves with not one but two champions. The roadshow had reached the city of Philadelphia when Bob received a telegram summoning him to his wife s bedside. Rose had been taken ill, and the show was immediately wound up, as Fitz dashed back to New York. By the time he reached her, the love of his life and mother of his children had taken a turn for the worse.

After a full-scale emergency in which the frantic husband summoned doctor after doctor to their Bath Beach home, it became painfully apparent that his actions were in vain. Rose never regained consciousness, and passed away quietly before her tearful family s eyes. Sitting by her bedside, Bob could only watch in despair as his wife ebbed away before him, too ill to say goodbye.

Fitzsimmons immediately sank from what had been the glorious highs of his action-adventure life to the very blackest depths of despair. He was transformed from the out-going life and soul of any party to a helpless shell of a man. Reports say he was devastated by the loss to the extent that he appeared to be giving up on life altogether, indulging in self-destructive drinking bouts and violent mood swings, as he found himself haunted by his worst demons. He and Rose been married just under ten years, and in that time he d gone from promising young hopeful to all-conquering champion. This was due, in no small part, to her unwavering support, which not only manifested itself in her vocal ringside encouragement, but in their private life, when the often wild and erratic showman needed guidance, direction, and most of all, love. It was to her that he d looked after beating James Corbett in a viciously fought battle. It was on her that he lavished fulsome praise at every opportunity. And it was she who tearfully defended the ageing prizefighter when he had been so cruelly cut down by the fearsome fists of Jim Jeffries. They had a relationship which few would understand amidst the mercenary, cut-throat world of boxing, and yet it was precisely this anchor that allowed Bob to make his way through such perennially choppy waters.

While Bob was left without a soul-mate, their three young children were left without their loving mother. Eight-year-old Martin, six-year-old Robert Junior and four-year-old Rosalie now had only their father to turn to, and it was he who had the job of explaining to them that the woman who d lit up the Bensonhurst residence would be lighting it up no more. As well as losing his life-partner, Fitzsimmons had lost the steadying hand on the tiller which controlled the direction in which he was going, and how he was going to get there. Without Rose, there was a very real danger that the old fighter would lose all sense of purpose. Within a few months, the first signs of this would become all too obvious.

With golden-blonde hair and pale-blue eyes, Julia May Gifford was undoubtedly the star of the show. Her stunningly beautiful looks were only matched by a voice which enchanted all who heard it. The twenty-two-year-old actress seemed set for bigger and better things than the musical play she was currently appearing in at a Chicago theatre. Entitled *When Johnny Comes Marching Home*, it had been moderately received by theatre-goers in the Windy City. For one particular member of the audience, however, appreciation for the show s leading lady went far beyond polite applause — so much so that he returned every night for a week to take in the heady charms of the young woman. She may have been slightly surprised to discover that her admirer was none other than the former world heavyweight champion, Robert Fitzsimmons. If so, she soon overcame her astonishment, as the two entered a whirlwind romance that saw them married only three months after his wife s death.

If the new Mrs Fitzsimmons hadn t yet caught her breath, she soon had plenty of time in which to do so, as her husband was summoned with his new bride to Jim Jeffries training camp in California, where the former boiler-maker was preparing to once more enter the ring with Jim Corbett.

Whether or not it was the effect of having Fitzsimmons among his seconds, Jeffries knocked out Corbett in ten rounds, to the undoubted satisfaction of the Cornishman, who still bore a smouldering grudge against his old rival. A bemused Julia May— who was accustomed to a rather more cerebral social circle — may have had time to reflect on her rather hasty marriage, as the honeymoon-cum-training session meant she saw very little of her new partner.

This is possibly just as well, if his romantic surprise during their wedding breakfast is anything to go by. According to an article compiled by a Cornish Women s Institute, Fitzsimmons proved he fell far short of the standards required of an ideal husband, when he revealed to his bride an enormous painting which he d commissioned and which now enjoyed pride of place on their drawing-room wall. It seems the subject of the life-size portrait was none other than Julia s predecessor in the marital home, the late Rose, smiling out over her former domain in all her glory. The new Mrs Fitzsimmons s reaction to this horrendous faux pas isn t included in the essay, but it seems unlikely that she would have been enraptured to see this particular work of art. As if this crass blunder hadn t provided sufficient warning, in the coming months Julia was to learn more about the unpredictable nature of life with the eccentric Cornishman, not to mention the responsibility of looking after his three young children. While she was coming to terms with her new-found status as a celebrity s wife, her spouse was in turn trying to come to terms with the fact that with his advancing years and fading form, he was no longer the celebrity he d once been. An opportunity was soon to present itself, which appeared to give Fitz the chance to reclaim some of his former glory. With his wife returning to her career on the stage, it s likely that he was growing more discontent with sitting around the house, and was yearning for a return to the days of hard-fought blood and sweat.

A new division had just been created in boxing; the light-heavyweight class, which had been originally known in Britain as the cruiserweight class. A challenge was issued to Bob which would see him taking on the world champion at this weight, a man named George Gardner, from Massachusetts. Fitzsimmons was the underdog, but this time it wasn t merely due to his famed lack of size. Having passed the age of forty, and without a fight in almost eighteen months, the Cornishman was seen as washed-up — a fighter on the downslopes of what had been a great career. To remedy this misconception, Bob decided to get in some target practice. Some solid ring workouts would blow away the cobwebs and prove that the old magic was still there. Tragically, this logic would come true in a way which he could never have anticipated. His warm-up match saw him take on a man named Con Coughlin, with the intention that he should feel his way back into the art, finding his feet in time for what would surely be the big comeback.

In the event, the fight was stopped during the first round, when Coughlin caught a Fitzsimmons right-hand jab on the point of his chin, and immediately crumpled into an unconscious heap on the canvas. Events took a turn for the worse when the 33-year-old Irishman couldn t be revived and had to be carried from the ring. He was rushed to hospital, where he lapsed into a coma. Without regaining consciousness, he died the next day. Once again, Fitz was ultimately responsible for ending another man s life in the prize-ring. It s a macabre coincidence that both men who died in this way at his hands shared the same Christian name. In this case, as before, Bob was eventually cleared of all blame when it was found that Coughlin had been suffering from a severe heart condition, and certainly shouldn t have been fighting professionally. All the same, it was the last thing Fitz needed at a time when he was re-launching his professional career. The man s death preyed on his mind as the time drew near for his latest title challenge.

Fitzsimmons set about training at Alemada, near San Francisco, with such zeal that his ageing, battle-scarred body had begun to cry out in protest. Firstly, an enthusiastic running exercise almost ended up crippling him, as his feet became affected by terrible blistering which reduced his walking to a hobble. As if this weren t bad enough, he then insisted on taking long runs in heavy rain, presumably against all sensible advice to the contrary. Rather like a naughty child, his eagerness and enthusiasm would prove to be his own worst enemies. Predictably, he caught a heavy cold which, after two or three days, developed into a serious bout of pneumonia. Just as he had in the run-up to the second fight with Jeffries, the veteran was asking too much of his ageing body, with his overpowering will to win placing excessive demands on his stamina. Far from a lean fighting machine, the limping, cold-ridden fighter was a comical sight to behold as he doggedly continued his regular workouts. Passers-by were said to have been highly amused by the unusual gait of the athlete who passed them by on his training route, comparing him to a vaudeville performer. In the sparring ring, however, there was no place for laughter, as Fitzsimmons relentlessly laid into one fall guy after another to compensate for all the recent aggravation. Channelling and focusing his energy and determination, he was carefully refining his ringcraft while summoning extra reserves of strength into his deadly punching.

And if his walk was still slightly askew when he stepped through the ropes at the Mechanics Pavilion in San Francisco on the evening of 25 November 1903, it s unlikely that anyone noticed amid the thick tension which would have been hanging heavy in the night air. Even the final journey from training gym to ringside had still been strewn with hazards for Fitzsimmons. A doctor had flatly forbidden him to take part, on account of his ill-health. The Cornishman had to plead with the medic in order that the contest should take place. A mere $2,500 appearance fee would have almost certainly added some extra urgency to this argument. Professional pride was also at stake, however, as this not only represented an opportunity to claw his way back among boxing s ruling elite; it presented a handy opportunity to punish Gardner, who said that Fitzsimmons was over the metaphorical hill. The younger man was said to be confidently forecasting an easy victory for himself, and claimed the contest would be stopped within three rounds.

If Gardner had ever made such a rash statement, it was a very different contender who came out of his corner on that November evening. Hesitantly moving about the ring with his hands held out in front of him, he looked more like a man bracing himself to receive a sound beating, rather than someone preparing to administer one. Fitzsimmons later remarked: I have never quite made up my mind whether I was more ashamed of him for being so frightened, than I was disgusted. Like hounds close to the scent of a fox, the audience had come to see battle commence, and immediately detected the distinct lack of bloodlust in the air. Groans and hisses filled the auditorium as they realised Gardner wasn t giving his all, while a stern telling-off from Fitzsimmons also seemed to have little or no effect, Don t you know where you are . . . why don t you fight? scolded the Cornishman in a theatrical stage whisper. It seemed as if the worlds of theatre and sport had coincided, as the pair carried on the charade for several more minutes and the crowd poured scorn on the pantomime with cries of Fake!

A half-hearted attempt at a punch from Gardner came only after encouragement from his exasperated opponent and even then the result was laughable, falling feebly short of the intended target. Perhaps it was his reputation, but Fitz appeared to have actually scared the other man into almost certain defeat. Clearly this was the last thing his own comeback campaign needed — a charade from which no-one would emerge with his dignity intact. An episode which had started badly soon got even worse as endless prancing around began to take its toll on Fitzsimmons s feet. He was forced to continue the fight standing only on his heels, as the pain of the blisters pulled him up short when he tried to move freely. The spectacle of one fighter too terrified to punch, and the other unable to walk properly, only added to the audience s displeasure. An ominous sign could be seen in the second round, when a gentle warm-up jab succeeded in knocking Gardner off his feet, much to Fitzsimmons s apparent surprise. Unfortunately for him, he broke one of his own knuckles in the process, no doubt adding to his discomfort. As he fought on, the hand began swelling up inside the glove, sending arrows of pain up his entire arm. By the third round, however, the comedy of errors seemed to have subsided, and proceedings took a more professional footing. Gardner even conquered his stage-fright sufficiently to perform a little footwork and generally start to size up his opponent properly. The fourth round brought the first knockdown, as a left-hand punch sent Gardner reeling to the floor. He regained his composure quickly enough to climb to his feet within the count. For the first time, a real exchange ensued, with the pair trading lively blows in one of the corners.

Unfortunately, yet another medical mishap was awaiting Fitzsimmons. A weighty blow delivered to Gardner s bobbing head landed with enough force to break another knuckle on his already injured hand. It says a lot of the forty-year-old veteran that he was even able to continue the contest, despite the excruciating pain in his hands and feet. Such was his experience, though, that he was seemingly able to make every shot count, stamping his authority on the fight and thoroughly unsettling his opponent. In the opening seven rounds, Gardner was knocked down a total of seven times and each time he came back for more. Fitz later claimed that each of these seven knockdowns caused further damage to his own hands, but he determined that he would finally get the better of the other man, as he felt himself to be the deserving winner. The bout became more and more of a wrestling match, as the two pushed and pulled, grappled and grabbed, as limbs tangled and bodies clashed, while the crowd excitedly continued to urge both men forward. By this time, Gardner had fully redeemed himself as a man of some courage, fighting on with part of one ear missing, while Fitzsimmons s various ailments really began to tell. Fatigue gradually overtook them both. After an exhausting twenty rounds the points decision went to Fitzsimmons by a significant margin. It was with some relief that he survived the duration, as he later confessed that his pneumonia and other assorted medical problems would have laid him low, had Gardner landed some punches on him. This mood of unassuming modesty didn t last long. He later went on to boast that if he had been fully fit, Gardner would have been lucky to survive the first round.

Bob s advancing years meant that his hold on the light-heavyweight world title — while impressive — was by no means a long-term arrangement. It had provided another highlight of a career which spanned three decades, but time was fast running out and he knew it. His last official title was finally taken from him two years later at the famous Mechanics Pavilion in San Francisco by Jack O Brien. The attendance at the venue proved the veteran could still draw a crowd, yet many also would have been keen to see O Brien in action, as he was regarded as one of the most promising stars of the time.

The two men had met on the canvas before, in a six-round exhibition bout staged in Philadelphia during the previous year. It s likely that Fitzsimmons regarded O Brien as a strong potential threat, while O Brien knew from his personal experience that while the old man had slowed up considerably he was still capable of packing a nasty punch. When they touched gloves in earnest this time, however, spectators were reminded that the champion wouldn t see forty again. Fitzsimmons appeared to have weakened significantly since the epic battles with Corbett and Jeffries. It was these very conflicts which had reduced his hands to misshapen lumps, as the effects of thousands of hard punches had made them brittle and tender. Rheumatism had set in where the bones were weak, rendering him unable to fight with anything like his former vigour. With Fitzsimmons visibly tiring, O Brien caught him with stinging blows to the face and body, each of which rocked the champion back on his heels. The Cornishman s timing had been so badly impaired that when a swinging punch slewed wide of its target, the momentum caused him to fall flat on his face. A once-great fighter had now taken on the appearance of a has-been, living only on the memories of greater things. The saying that the spirit is willing but the flesh is weak was beginning to ring true, as the veteran gamely defended his title with a spirited flurry of blows. But there was only ever going to be one winner.

Calls from the ringside urged O Brien to show the older man mercy and finish him off, so the defeated man could escape with some dignity. The challenger duly obliged, with a strong clip to the face that sent Fitzsimmons sprawling to the floor, but the Cornishman shakily struggled to his feet and fought grimly on. He even managed to get in a few punches of his own, as if delivering a reminder to all present that he had once been a world-class contender. Just as Fitz himself had defeated the ageing Dempsey at the outset of his career, it was now time for the new guard to take over. Bob s growing weariness was apparent by the end of the twelfth round, when sheer exhaustion meant he could barely defend himself. The thirteenth round saw him take yet more agonising punishment, and he subsequently slipped from his stool during the break at the end of it. His head lolling on his chest, he admitted he could fight no more, and his seconds finally threw in the towel. The fight was over, in more ways than one. This was the end.

When he d been revived, Fitzsimmons publicly announced his retirement from the ring. Echoing his words after the Jeffries fight, he swore he d never climb into a ring again.

While Fitzsimmons s career was touching rock-bottom, his personal problems were rapidly reaching dizzy new heights. In true soap-opera style, just days after the curtain had fallen on his disastrous performance in the ring at San Francisco, he received a telegram from New York. It was from his beautiful young wife, coldly and matter-of-factly informing him that their marriage was over.

The attraction had always been obtuse — the beautiful young actress and the hard-bitten prizefighter. She was a delicate rose, he an unprepossessing thorn. From the moment she was whisked away from the theatre stage to join the blood-and-sweat atmosphere of a Californian training camp, the former Ms Gifford can have been under no illusions as to the new life she was undertaking. The seemingly undue haste of their courtship was a puzzlement to many. It s highly unlikely that she would have been attracted by Bob s clean-cut good looks, as all too frequent poundings in the ring had left an indelible mark on his rugged features which, in truth, weren t too handsome to begin with. It s possible she may have been carried away by the glamour of life in the public spotlight. But whereas Bob had once been drunk on the heady wine of fame, as his career declined he was now draining its last bitter dregs. He and Rose — whom many maintained would always be the true love of his life — had enjoyed the glory years, when he was the all-conquering hero, but Julia had unknowingly arrived when Bob was facing a very different future, having reached an age where he could no longer compete at the highest level. This may have been a major factor in the stormy relationship which ensued, as his wife complained that Bob was fast becoming ill at ease with himself, clearly frustrated by his enforced lifestyle. It was a lifestyle which was positively sedate, compared to the days of climbing in and out of prize-rings around the United States. A possible catalyst in their whirlwind romance may simply have been that she found him good company. Admittedly, the old rogue did possess charm and also boasted a ready wit, which was often called upon in his role of after-dinner speaker at a number of major social occasions.

Whatever the basis for their relationship, it soon became abundantly clear that all was far from rosy, especially when Julia formed a close friendship with a theatre company manager for whom she worked. That gentleman, Charles Sibley, was understandably alarmed when newspapers speculated about his role as a third party in the Fitzsimmons marriage. No doubt reflecting on his supposed love rival s prowess with his fists, Sibley strenuously denied the allegations. He did so all the more emphatically when Fitz — with a characteristic sense of the dramatic — actually challenged him to a duel. It s unlikely, however, that Julia was actually having an affair — a far more likely explanation is that Fitzsimmons was merely obsessively jealous of his wife s accquaintances.

Observers described relations between the couple as tempestuous while enforced absences because of respective engagements hardly helped. When Julia announced she was leaving, Bob pursued her across the country, eventually tracking her down in Sioux City, Iowa. In a dramatic denouement worthy of one of the actress s plays, he managed to talk her out of divorcing him, whereupon the couple returned to their new home — a farm in the state of New Jersey, which the boxer apparently planned to turn into a health resort. While the reunion seemed to hold, the marriage remained on rocky ground.

Throughout their troubles, they did seem to retain something in common: their abiding love for the stage. They appeared together in a new version of Bob s play, *A Man s A Man*, playing to packed houses across the United States. Dates in Australia and New Zealand followed with similar success, with Bob enjoying a nostalgic trip to the stamping grounds of his youth. The tour was topped off in style by another visit to England, where they performed in London and Birmingham, once more to great acclaim. It was during this latest visit to his homeland that Bob met up again with Jem Mace, who was now in his late seventies. The man who introduced the shy young blacksmith to the world of professional fighting certainly had a lot of catching up to do with his former prot g . It was around this time that Bob admitted that he felt his future lay on the stage, as he could no longer rely on his fighting abilities to earn a living. A disastrous and short-lived return to the ring would only serve to confirm the wisdom of this rare moment of reason — he foolishly agreed to take on black boxer Jack Johnson in a six-round fight in Philadelphia.

Johnson was greatly feared for his colossal strength, weighing in as one of the new breed of powerful heavyweights. He was also generally rated as one of the best all-round fighters since the Corbett-Sullivan era, combining two-handed punching power with an awesome strength. Known as the Galveston Giant, in honour of the Texas town where he was born in 1878, he stood over six feet in height, weighing just under two hundred pounds. As we ve heard through his meeting with Jim Jeffries, it was Johnson who inspired the phrase Great White Hope as US promoters tried desperately

DEATH ... AND MARRIAGE

to find a white man who could conquer the black champion. Many boxers were soundly thumped in their bid for this dubious accolade, with Johnson s reign lasting until 1915, when the fondness he d developed for the good life finally caught up with him. He was knocked out by the six-foot cowboy Jess Willard in a contest staged in Havana, Cuba. His meteoric rise to fame co-incided with the demise of Fitzsimmons s own fortunes and the twenty-nine-year-old Texan was considered to be in his prime when he was pitted against the fading Cornishman.

If those around him had tried to talk the middle-aged veteran out of trying to make yet another comeback, they failed, for he gamely faced the young giant on 17 July 1907 at the Washington Athletic Club. Modern-day boxing boards would never have permitted the ill-matched pairing to take place, with the former champion now in his forty-fourth year and Johnson triumphantly dealing out some vicious beatings on his route to the top-flight. Besides his age, there was another handicap would have impeded Bob considerably. It transpired that he had been indulging in horseplay while training, and had torn the ligaments clean away from his elbow. A bandage had been fitted, but infected fluid was draining from the limb via a specially-fitted tube. Aside from the physical discomfort this must have caused, it would hardly have instilled much confidence in his chances, if indeed there was still anyone brave enough to back him. Fitzsimmons claimed he was more than able to fight and that the injury wasn t troubling him, but he was about to regret those rash words.

The referee was understandably alarmed at the sight of what appeared to be a fighter with a broken arm, but after a quick medical examination had established this wasn t the case, the bout — amazingly — was allowed to continue. Not that it continued for very long. A hard shot from the old man slammed into Johnson s side, just like the old days, but rather than causing the victim to wince in pain as it once would have done, it merely drew a condescending laugh from the young giant. Fitzsimmons certainly wasn t laughing when he immediately caught a return blow around the head that knocked him sideways. Ten years before, he would have seen it coming. Twenty years before, he would have been beating a lively rhythm on Johnson s head by now. Once more, the man who d become a legend of the ring two decades ago appeared to be outstaying his welcome in it. Becoming more and more farcical by the minute, the fight continued until the next round, with Johnson battering Fitz at will, with the latter seemingly powerless to do anything about it. Punches reeled off at random cannoned into Fitz around the head and body, lurching him from side to side. The younger man even seemed to be playing with his victim, much like a cat toys with its intended prey. Even when the breathless veteran tried to hold his opponent in a clinch, he was effortlessly flung to the floor, rather like a doll cast aside by a child. Mercifully, the shameful spectacle came to a close before the end of that round, when a right hook from Johnson knocked Fitzsimmons flat on his back, where he lay motionless with his feet sticking straight up in the air. A pitiful attempt to get up ended with him slumping forward onto the canvas, where he lay face down, dead to the world. Boos and hisses fell upon the ring as the crowd voiced their displeasure, while seconds revived the conquered fighter. Memories of former glory days were fading fast, rapidly being replaced with images like these — images which were both undignified and embarrassing to all who witnessed them.

Despite the fact that he could obviously no longer compete on equal terms with the best in the business, the forty-five-year-old defiantly proved that he could still hold his own against the average bully. At a region by the name of Benson Mines, near the border with Canada, a young firebrand had reputedly proved himself to be the top fighter, gaining something of a fearful reputation. It seemed that he d beaten numerous colleagues from the local timber industry in a series of impromptu prizefights. The bully s name was Jim Paul and when his workmates heard that Bob Fitzsimmons was visiting the area with a touring play, they contacted the former world champion, and asked him to step into the roped square once more. It says much of the level to which Fitz had sunk that he agreed to such a scheme, although it s possible that his pride would have made the invitation impossible to refuse in any case. Cheers from the assembled timber-workers filled the air as the middle-aged fighter was led into the ring. Itinerant labourers roared their appreciation as the game old pro raised his fists in that familiar straight-backed pose one more time, in order to test his mettle against the young tough. There was life in the old dog yet. And he taught the raw rookie a much-needed lesson of experience over enthusiasm. Despite the age difference, Bob showed he had lost few of his former skills, jabbing sharply at the younger man s head in a classic exhibition of old-fashioned prizefighting. A well-timed stinging clip around the ear was enough to send Paul crashing down into the dust. A second punch was enough to swiftly end the fight as the humiliated Paul staggered and sank back to the dirt once more. A standing ovation marked Fitzsimmons s efforts as he left the ring. It was a triumph of age over youth.

Small triumphs aside, the generally downward spiral of his fighting career can have done little to ease Bob s frame of mind at this time, especially when coupled with growing domestic strife and ever more acute money problems. Clearly, there would be no more golden purses from big-money fights. It was around this time that Julia claimed her husband began to seek full-time solace in the bottom of a whisky bottle. Having largely abstained for most of his life due to the demands of his profession, he certainly now began to imbibe rather more than was good for him. It was a habit which developed over the next few years, she said, as he found little else in the outside world to offer him comfort from his many troubles. She later claimed that during this time Bob had physically attacked her on more than one occasion, throwing bottles at her in a drunken rage and threatening to shoot her. It was a charge he hotly denied, countering with accusations that she d deliberately bled him dry financially. He claimed that she d received around $200,000 worth of clothes and jewellery, along with around $100,000 in cash — staggering sums which would equate to millions in today s financial environment. Somewhat predictably, their marriage would finally end in divorce, after twelve years and numerous estrangements and reconciliations. But if anyone thought Bob was about to bow quietly out of public life after this and other recent episodes, they would have been very much mistaken.

15. One Fight too Many

Sydney, Australia
Boxing Day 1909

The dominant male of an animal pack lives under constant threat. A successful coup from within the ranks will claim his position and his life. For an athlete at the peak of his or her profession, the struggle for supremacy is admittedly less hazardous, but remains just as clearly defined. And for those who fall ignominiously from grace, the outcome can often seem just as harsh. A professional fighter — like that dominant male — can only continue to reign if he s capable of physically overpowering all in his pack who would take his crown. In both worlds, there s a constant supply of challengers.

This law of the jungle scenario was about to be played out as spectators crowded into the large sports arena on the outskirts of Sydney. Survival of the fittest — the gnarled, battle-scarred veteran who lives off his reputation, challenged by the newly-blooded young buck. A gentlemanly version of the age-old battle for supremacy. The fashionable sporting event which would decide the Heavyweight Prizefighting Championship of Australia was a reminder that time is the major catalyst in our theory. Like an ageing madam hiding her mottled complexion with heavy make-up, boxing was trying to cleanse its present . . . and deny its past. Dusty warehouses and bare, bloody knuckles had long since given way to bright white canvas and padded leather gloves. Tramps and triggermen, cowboys and con-artists — the undesirable elements traditionally associated with the noble art — they were now ghosts of far-off days; their shouts and jeers fading to a distant echo. In their place were the beautiful people — a middle-class clique who dictated the social calendar of the day, counting well-known actors, musicians and other celebrities among their illustrious numbers.

Today, for example, well-dressed men and women relax on the seats which span back to the far walls of the open-air auditorium.

Of course, the reason these people came to the fights was exactly the same as that of their rather more disreputable predecessors; namely, to watch two men hit each other in the face until one is knocked to the ground. The audience and the theatre may have changed, but the play remained very much the same. This changing of the seasons was also evident at the ringside. An unbribeable referee and an equally impartial timekeeper were in shirt-sleeved attendance, flanked by doctors and first-aid men. Persuaded out of retirement one last time, Fitzsimmons s battered profile and disfigured hands were a physical reminder of an age when such social niceties hadn t even been considered, let alone observed. But if these measures were intended to sterilise the air of savagery which exists when two powerful men physically attack each other, they failed on all counts. A yet more telling development was the Kinetoscope which whirred at the corner of the ring, an important component in boxing s move into a new age of entertainment. Today s contest would be recorded for posterity, on what Fitz called movin pitchers . The distribution of money from the proceeds of these pitchers had already been the subject of heated debate among boxers, who felt they were too often deprived of their share. Inevitably, Bob was among those who d shouted loudest and longest on this sensitive topic. Throughout his lengthy career, he spent as much time battling promoters as he did opponents. Although he wouldn t live to see it, his successors in the sport would continue the same debate over the next hundred years.

As he prepared for battle, it was clear that the Cornishman had also been personally affected by the passing of time. While he still boasted the lean, muscled body of a streetfighter it was undeniably that of a forty-six-year-old streetfighter. His thin legs seemed frail and spindly, as though likely to collapse under the sheer force of his opponent s power. His bald head and lived-in features gave him the rather engaging air of a sprightly grandfather, vainly trying to recapture his misspent youth at a fairground boxing booth. This fight was indeed the professional equivalent of that winner-takes-all boxing booth, as Bob was now reduced to wringing the last few dollars from the sport, since his defeat at the hands of O Brien had brought his career to an end. As if to reinforce the generation gap, the muscular young man in the opposite corner began skipping effortlessly from one foot to another, moving in an easy, smooth rhythm as the crowd murmured in anticipation. Twenty years his junior, Big Bill Lang was everything Bob used to be. Youthful, strong — and very much aware of both facts. He was noticeably bigger and heavier than the older man, with broad-beam shoulders and huge, ham-like arms. Standing over six feet tall, he weighed in at an impressive fourteen stone four pounds, with the tightly-knit muscles across his chest and arms reinforcing his reputation as a big hitter. William Langfranci hailed from Melbourne, and in a five-year professional career had already claimed the heavyweight title of Australia. Although he hadn t yet fought outside the country, he had suffered a defeat at the hands of Jack Johnson two years before — one of only two defeats on his record.

The time leading up to the contest was busy for Fitzsimmons as he glad-handed his way around Sydney, performing a series of public engagements and celebrity appearances — every inch the returning hero. He even acted as referee in a number of local boxing tournaments and exhibitions, while illuminating each occasion with his sheer presence. He also gave a talk on physical culture to a group of Sydney policemen, entertaining them with demonstrations of how he d achieved his most famous victories in the ring.

But on the day itself, there was real work to be done. A buzz ran through the crowd as the gladiators prepared to do battle. The combined air of excitement and danger could be felt throughout the arena, as the expectation of physical conflict reached a noisy peak. The crowd, who d abandoned Christmas festivities for the sake of this bout, rooted fairly and squarely for the old warrior, urging him to turn on the old magic one last time. An observer would have taken a rather different view from the outset. Fitz seemed to shrink in size as the men both came out of their corners. Psychologically, the visible age difference seemed to have introduced a third opponent to the ring; one which had worn the veteran fighter down with more ruthless efficiency than any mere man he d ever faced. As his glory days faded, Fitzsimmons was finally in danger of being well and truly defeated — by his own advancing years. With his trademark white breeches adorning his equally famous gait, Fitz once more assumed the slightly awkward stance which had graced prizefighting rings from New York City to the Rio Grande. Hips thrust forward, fists held high, his chin defiant. With the air of a soldier going forth from the trenches, he moved purposefully across the ring.

His eyes already closed, the Cornishman s sweat-soaked head slammed against the canvas with sickening force, spraying a fine mist of blood and perspiration across the floor of the ring. A vicious blow had felled him like a slaughtered animal. The slain warrior twitched convulsively as he came to rest. Lying motionless and helpless, he looked as if he d been hit by a truck. The m l e threatened to boil over as the crowd s angry roars reached new heights. It was still clear with which corner they sided; boos and jeers rained on the broad shoulders of their hapless countryman. Meanwhile, the focus of their attention was currently standing over his prey, like a hunter approaching a fallen stag. His menacing presence served as an irrefutable statement that his opponent was safer staying where he was.

When Lang had stepped into the ring, respect for his vastly-experienced adversary appeared to have been deliberately set aside along with his warming-up gown. Indeed, he may have feared that mere acknowledgement of Fitzsimmons s legendary career would blunt the cutting edge of his own attack. Well-practised moves from the former world champion had only served as delaying tactics, rather than genuine attacks. During the build-up to the fight, Lang was acutely aware of Fitzsimmons s history. He knew the man had fought his way from poverty in a far-off land called Cornwall to become one of the most famous sportsmen in the world — on first-name terms with the US president himself. Bob Fitzsimmons brought his awesome reputation with him every time he clambered between the ropes. The stories were endlessly re-told — mainly by Fitz himself, it must be said — he d fought bare-knuckled sideshow bouts with cowboys, he d been escorted into Western prizefighting rings at gunpoint. He d been refereed by Wyatt Earp, and guarded by Black Bat Masterson. But now he had finally been put down—possibly hurt and *certainly* defeated. Perhaps this train of thought flashed through Lang s mind in the dying seconds of the contest — it s more likely he was almost as stunned as his opponent.

By the time the victim had been lifted to his feet and revived into consciousness, the event was already over. As well as losing out on the prize money, Fitzsimmons had lost what standing he had left as a world-class professional fighter. On this occasion, he was a loser. The defeat also had wider implications — age was just one of the factors which would conspire to prevent him ever challenging for a title again.

There comes a point in everyone s life when they realise that this is as good as it s going to get. They re as fit, strong or smart as they re ever going to be. It seemed Fitz had long since reached that point, and was now fast descending the other side of the mountain. It was a very different man who now stood in his corner, having been lifted to his feet. Still dazed, he looked blankly around the arena as the significance of his humiliating defeat washed over him. It was as if Fitzsimmons, the showman, the entertainer who d brought his unique personality to the world stage, had now finally been cast aside with the other relics of early American prizefighting. Although his senses were numbed, his pride must have felt every cheer in the arena, as though it were another punch. He watched as Lang s arm was held aloft by the referee, with the Sydney crowd continuing to blame its home-grown champion for the fate which had befallen the world s favourite fighter. Reports tell how Fitzsimmons himself was moved to tears as he spoke to waiting reporters in the dressing-room. Struggling to overcome his emotions, he admitted that he was now clearly too old for the calling which had transformed his life and made him a star. He said that the day s events had made him painfully aware of this fact, in a way that he hadn t fully realised before. I am satisfied this is the end, he said. I couldn t rough it with that big, strong, husky young fellow. He went on: How I longed for the old vigour, the strength and speed that enabled me to hit hard when I got the chance and keep pace with my opponent no matter how fast he fought. His aides comforted him and told him the hot sun was to blame. But

Bob knew the truth, and after all the reporters had gone, he would have been left alone with the knowledge of what had really happened, and why.

The king was dead. Long live the king.

Fitzsimmons and Lang met up again before the former went back to America. This time the surroundings were rather more convivial. Lang presented the man he d beaten with a gold cardcase, as an award for his gentlemanly conduct throughout his visit. The presentation took place at a boxing show in Sydney, and was also meant to signify a tribute for the contribution Bob had made to the world of boxing over the past three decades. Fitz thanked the young man and made an effusive speech of gratitude for the hospitality which had been heaped apon him since his arrival. Repeating that he was now retired as a fighter, he received a resounding ovation as he left the ring. Later that night, the two men continued their pleasantries at Bob s hotel, along with Billy Williams, Lang s manager. The revelry continued into the wee small hours as Fitzsimmons held court before his enthralled guests. The young Lang was particularly captivated by the living history of his chosen sport being re-lived before his eyes. Like a father to his son, the ageing veteran even demonstrated some of his favourite tricks of the trade, with the Australian as his apt pupil. Although this particular episode thus ended on a high note, it also served as a further reminder that Fitzsimmons s glory days were very much in the past, and could only live on in story form.

The unspeakable had finally happened. The king had long since lost his crown and he was now unable to challenge anyone else ever again. Fitzsimmons bemoaned this, his final fate, claiming in hindsight that he should never have stepped into the ring with the fearsome Lang. In an interview soon after the fight, the ex-champion emphatically stated once more that he certainly had no intention of taking up the gloves again and that he was retired for good. Nevertheless, it would no doubt have been a statement welcomed by those family and friends who cared for his interests. Any impartial observer at the unholy exhibition in Sydney would have seen a middle-aged man trying vainly to defend himself against a younger, stronger adversary. Rather than a competitive sporting bout, it had resembled an alleyway mugging, with Fitzsimmons cast as the helpless victim. A referee s count wasn t needed.

The fight was the most telling indication yet of just how far Fitzsimmons had fallen from the champions league he once dominated. It showed the perils of carrying on way past your personal shelf life, for purely financial reasons. Film footage of the fight tells a sad story. There can be few more pitiful sights than that of the ageing veteran being bombarded relentlessly by the muscular Lang in those last few moments before mercifully tumbling to the floor. Ironically, every fight he took on now devalued his personal stock even further, as people realised he was a pale shadow of the dynamic force he d once been. He blamed the onset of age, cursing the sapped strength and lack of vigour which now bedevilled him in contests he would once have mastered. His hands, broken so many times on the skulls of defeated opponents, had been permanently damaged as a result of his own formerly deadly power. Now, his knuckles and fists were misshapen and fragile. A thrown punch was likely to hurt him as much as its intended victim. To the rest of us, this is scarcely surprising. A man approaching his fiftieth birthday cannot hope to summon the same physical fervour as that of his younger self, and the overwhelming strain placed on Fitzsimmons s body by more than 350 arduous battles would have accelerated the ageing process immeasurably. It was a brutal fact that he just couldn t cut it any more. It was time to retire, before he became a washed-up has-been, tarnishing the glory he once revelled in. To carry on in the face of this undeniable situation would be to contravene the laws of nature, and those who would try to do this are merely deceiving themselves.

In a personal insight to his psyche, Fitz himself graphically described the bitter frustration he faced during these fading twilight years of his career. He said that whereas a punch thrown by him a few years earlier would have consigned an opponent to the canvas, now it would only have a limited effect and he himself had neither the pace nor the stamina to avoid the riposte which would surely follow. He claimed to have noticed the difference which was now evident in his famous training runs; where before he could boast that he d run the legs off his companions, now his own legs would force him to bring the run to a premature end. Mind over matter is a popular theory of positive thinking. But there are limits.

Fitzsimmons had almost certainly borne the fast-approaching mortality of his fighting career in mind some years earlier, when he made an attempt to cast his net rather wider in the field of professional sport. This was presumably done in the hope of prolonging his spell in the public eye and reinforcing the fame he d already enjoyed as a boxer. After all, to the man formerly known as Fighting Bob , the chance to appear before an audience — any audience — was the stuff of life itself. It s always important to know your limits, and to remain within those boundaries where sensible, in order to avoid making a complete fool of yourself. Friends would almost certainly have pressed Fitzsimmons on this matter, as he prepared to join the world of wrestling. But the theory of common sense had no meaning in the personal world inhabited by Fitz, and he would merely have scoffed at anyone foolish enough to try preaching caution to him.

On the face of it, it may not have seemed such a bad idea at first. For a man who d long been renowned as one of the best fighters on the planet, a physical contest of strength in a roped ring wouldn t have seemed far removed from his own field of expertise. The canvas square held no fears for him, after all. But in reality, there was a world of difference, and it was only Fitzsimmons s childlike enthusiasm for showing off and entertaining the public that led him to believe he could survive, let alone triumph, in a wrestling ring. Wrestlers use their size, weight and strength to intimidate opponents; they use a variety of techniques to throw, pin or hold. While Fitz could, at his peak, hit harder than almost any man in boxing, he obviously lacked the stature or presence for a contest of this kind, while possessing next to none of the necessary skills. It s likely he may have had some flirtation with the Cornish wrestling of his home county, as his elder brother Jarrett was a promising exponent of the traditional pastime; but apart from playful wrestles with his pet lion Nero in the run-up to big fights, Fitz was rather lacking in both qualifications and experience. The nearest he d come in recent years was a rowdy backstage scuffle with Jim Jeffries before their title fight, following an argument about the rules of clinching and releasing. Jeffries graphically demonstrated how he d react to illegal holding by bodily picking up the Cornishman in his huge arms and hurling him through the air across the dressing-room, whereupon he slammed into a wall and slid to the ground, dazed. His slight frame was no match for the burly Jeffries, and there was no reason to believe this wrestling match would be any different.

In fairness, the opponent chosen for this ill-advised enterprise wasn t a wrestler himself, but a fellow boxer. He was Gus Ruhlin, the same man Fitzsimmons had beaten so convincingly in the run-up to the second Jeffries fight. It had been Ruhlin s backers who d actually suggested the meeting, as Gus s own career was on the skids, and he needed money. Ruhlin s manager Billy Madden met up with Fitz back in 1901 to sow the seed of the hair-brained scheme, and he found Fitzsimmons a willing listener. The match would be staged at Madison Square Garden, and it would be advertised as a star attraction, in the hope of attracting boxing fans to the unusual pairing. The intention was that of a good-natured, fair contest which would capture the imagination of the paying public, as they would have the chance to see two professional fighters try their hand at a ring discipline which was alien to both of them. And so, when the two eventually met up on the canvas, it was with a slightly awkward grace that they moved about the ring, each with arms held wide in order to grapple their opponent as they d been taught.

Of course, it was bound to end in tears. The only surprise was the comparatively short length of time it took for the spectacle to descend into a riotous brawl. The spark that ignited the ever-present fuse was an unintentional clash of heads which left Ruhlin bleeding heavily from a facial cut. The spirit of fair play immediately evaporated and war was summarily declared, with Fitzsimmons landing a hefty punch in his opponent s groggy face. Here were two powerful men, well-versed in the noble art, now unleashed on each other with bare-knuckles and evil intent. To his credit, referee Charley White tried his best to restore order, but

Fitzsimmons s blood was up, and he pushed the official out of the way in order to launch himself on Ruhlin. Both men now waded into one another, trading punches and careering around the ring, totally out of control. Fists cracked sharply as the shots went home much to the delight of the audience, who were hysterical at witnessing the full-blooded bare-knuckle contest this had become. Ruhlin grabbed hold of Fitzsimmons and dragged him to the floor, where they rolled over in an untidy heap. The two tussled on the canvas for some minutes, like schoolboys in a playground. Eventually they extricated themselves and jumped to their feet, where they resumed hostilities once more, again swapping potentially lethal punches in an ever more frantic exchange. The torsos of both men were smeared with blood, and each looked as if he d narrowly survived a particularly vicious bar brawl. As they paused for breath, Ruhlin launched himself on Fitz, pushing him to the ground and hurling himself down on top of him. Winded, the Cornishman was unable to throw his opponent off and duly conceded the first fall. If he was angry before, Bob was beside himself with rage by now and cursed loudly from his corner during the rest between rounds. When they came forth once more, the referee redoubled his efforts to enforce the wrestling rules, and dissipate the uncontrolled violence of the previous session.

He might as well have saved his breath. Fitzsimmons drove an agonising punch into Ruhlin s mid-section, duplicating the famous strike which had once felled Jim Corbett for the world title. This time, while the recipient doubled up in pain, he was able to continue; proof indeed that the famous punch, and indeed the boxer who had dealt it with a bare fist, no longer possessed their former power. In retaliation, Gus grabbed Fitz in a choke-hold, squeezing his throat and forcing him back, while the Cornishman frantically fought for breath. Breaking free, he thrust a furious left-hand strike into Ruhlin s side, causing him to gasp and stumble away. As Fitzsimmons desperately tried to regain his breath, however, his opponent came back at him once more, this time picking him bodily from the ground and holding him high in the air. His brawny arms threw the struggling blacksmith down onto the floor with a slam, which well and truly knocked the last wind from Bob s sails. Dropping his weight on top of him, Ruhlin held the older man down to gain the second fall, and the match.

Aside from the obvious health hazards, neither fighter emerged from this dubious contest with his dignity intact, while Fitzsimmons in particular had spectacularly failed to cover himself in glory. Needless to say, his much-vaunted wrestling career came to an end, just as suddenly as it had begun.

After his recent string of humiliations, there seemed to be no choice for Bob but to hang up his gloves for good. So many times in the past few years had he proclaimed to wash his hands of the sport which had both deified and almost destroyed him. Each time he d been unable to resist the temptation to chance his arm just once more. By now, though, promoters had largely turned their back on him altogether, writing him off as a sad parody of his former self.

Astonishingly the year of 1914 saw him in action yet again, despite the fact that he was now just a few months away from his fifty-first birthday. Fight records describe a six-round exhibition bout in Williamsport — a favourite staging post back in days of old — paired him with a man named KO Sweeney. The ironically-initialled KO didn t live up to his name, however, as Fitzsimmons was able to last the distance, much to the approval of the crowd. A further bout in Pennsylvania saw our careworn hero travelling to the town of Bethlehem, where he laced up the gloves yet again, this time to face Jersey Bellew. Spectators were incredulous that the man gamely trading punches with Bellew was, in sporting terms, practically a pensioner. As all things come to an end, so this, finally, would be the last step in what had been a long and incredible journey. Although no-one present that evening knew it at the time, this fight would gain a special significance in the history of international sport, as it is the last-ever recorded appearance of Bob Fitzsimmons in a competitive boxing ring. He had, in a sense, come full circle; ending his career just as he had begun it, fighting second-rate journeymen in dingy halls for a few dollars. Never again would the awesome legend raise his gloves to another man in the name of professional fighting. But did this mean the old man had finally seen sense and willingly opted for a comfortable retirement? Not for a moment.

ONE FIGHT TOO MANY

It was a very different kind of battle in which Bob now found himself embroiled, and although no actual punches would be thrown, he was soon to discover the arena in which he was currently competing was every bit as tough and demanding as that of the prize ring. The man who d beaten countless opponents in middleweight, light-heavyweight and heavyweight title fights, was about to take on his most recent adversary, the Supreme Court of the United States of America. And, after some robust sparring and a number of vicious body blows, it looked as if the former champ was about to take a standing count. This latest contest had arisen from a much-publicised dispute with the New York Boxing Commission. Plans to stage a comeback, this time against Soldier Kearns, at the Atlantic Garden Athletic Club, had been well and truly scuppered by the sport s ruling body, who said — somewhat justifiably — that the fight would be unsafe, as the Cornishman was simply too old.

As if this wasn t damning enough, a ghost from Fitz s past had appeared in the opposing corner, backing the Boxing Commission s decision — John L Sullivan, once the bare-knuckled brawling champion of the US, now a rotund, white-bearded prohibition preacher and pillar of the community. The once famously bad-tempered bruiser couldn t resist adding the benefit of his own experience to the current debate, when he said it was ridiculous that a man of Fitzsimmons s age should be even contemplating a return to the ring. It was this that really seemed to get Bob s back up, as he and Sullivan had maintained a mutual dislike since their days of sporting rivalry. Many years before, a fight had been arranged between the two men, but the police had raided the secret location and prevented it from taking place. If the two middle-aged men had actually come face to face during this current war of newspaper print, it s likely they would have started where they d left off, such was the animosity over the highly-emotive issue. Fitzsimmons felt persecuted, he claimed, because he wasn t being given an opportunity to show that his old magic was still there. This meant, effectively, that he was being prevented from earning a living. The sport s officials obviously had the safety aspect in mind when they announced they wouldn t be giving him a licence, but they were also unlikely to have wanted to see the former champion make a fool of himself once more. It s likely that Sullivan, as an ex-champ, felt much the same way. Fitzsimmons, however, saw this as a case of sour grapes on Sullivan s part.

In the newspapers of the time, the Cornishman was famously quoted with all his usual finesse over this new difference of opinion:

> I have put up my own money against this verdict, but what gets my goat is for that old stiff, Sullivan, to come out in an interview saying that they have done right in putting the blinkers on me. What right has that fat old has-been to be telling the controlling body what they ought to do? Sullivan hasn t had a punch in him for donkey s years, but that s no reason why I should not be allowed to get in the ring and chase these white hope sprinters out of it.

One would have thought he d already said more than enough, but he continued: I suppose he [Sullivan] is still sore because I licked a vaudeville actor [a disparaging reference to Corbett] who put him to sleep. I guess he would like to see me shovelling up snow in the streets. All in all, a mastery of tact and understatement from the man who, although age prevented him from putting up a good fight, was more than prepared to talk one. The well-aimed shot across Sullivan s bows was gratefully lapped up by the press, to whom the halcyon days of warring prizefighters like Fitzsimmons, Sullivan and Corbett represented a golden age, where the men doing battle in the ring often did so simply because they didn t like each other. It s unlikely this outburst would have endeared him to boxing officials, or indeed put him in line for any form of diplomatic post within the sport.

In slating Sullivan, who hadn t climbed into a ring for nearly twenty years, Fitzsimmons drew attention to the fact that his own generation of fighters had all long since retired. In describing Corbett as a vaudeville actor , he denigrated his old rival for cashing in on his sporting prowess with lucrative theatrical engagements. This was rich coming from Fitzsimmons, who wasted no opportunity to tread the boards, if he thought there was money in it.

ONE FIGHT TOO MANY

At the subsequent appeal court hearing, Fitzsimmons duly rounded on the judge, insisting that he was more than fit enough to go back between the ropes, and could comfortably defeat a man half his age. The judge obviously wasn t convinced, as he ruled against Bob, upholding the Commission s decision. A desperate offer on behalf of the former champion to stage an exhibition bout there and then in the courtroom in order to display his fitness was politely — but firmly — declined. From that moment on, the veteran was barred for life from boxing within the entire New York State. Other bodies said they d take a similar line if he applied for a licence within their jurisdictions. Whether he liked it or not, Bob s career was over.

For an ever fickle public, the likes of Corbett and Fitzsimmons were now consigned to the history books. There were new heroes taking up the newspaper lineage that the Cornishman and his associates had dominated for so long. This became evident when the sport s distasteful obsession with finding a white man to knock out Jack Johnson proved fruitful within twelve months of Fitz s last fight. Big Jess Willard, an outsized cowboy from Kansas, proved himself equal to the task when he fought Johnson in Havana on 5 April 1915. Among the crowd who travelled to Cuba to see the fight was Fitzsimmons, now reduced to the role of spectator. Following intense press speculation, Willard confirmed himself as the new heavyweight champion of the world when he dumped the thirty-seven-year-old Johnson onto the canvas after no fewer than twenty-six hard-fought rounds. A new champion was born, and, like the constant changing of the seasons, another new era had begun.

16. In Retirement

While Fitzsimmons watched Willard wrestling the world title from Johnson s grasp, the former champion was left only with the memories of a time when he had held that coveted position. A huge part of his life had come to an end, as a result of being effectively barred from competitive boxing for life. It was almost certainly not the way he would have wanted to go; with a whimper, rather than a bang. It was an ignominious exit from the brutal world which had made him an international star, but along with his pressing financial commitments, it was perhaps within the nature of his character to keep battling when common sense would have compelled a lesser mortal to hang up his gloves.

The manner of his retirement, however, would never eclipse his achievements. In a career spanning more than three decades, he had faced around 369 opponents. It s generally thought that around 200 of these had only lasted the first few rounds. After graduating from the bloody school of bare-knuckle fighting, he had ridden the waves of boxing s growing popularity, establishing himself as one of its earliest ambassadors. His contribution would be remembered, as the sport continued its journey from the gutter to the parlour, with Fitzsimmons and his counterparts at the heart of its development. He had gained world championships at heavyweight, light-heavyweight and middleweight levels. He was the only fighter for the next thirty-five years to have won titles at three different weights. He d also staked a separate place in the record books — although he couldn t have known it at the time — as the only British-born undisputed heavyweight champion in history for the next 102 years. But most of all, the one-time blacksmith had put on a show. Geographically and spiritually, the young boy from Helston had come a long way, beating the best in the world as he went. From the Cornish tin-miners who d flocked to his fights in the desert, to the elegantly-clad sophisticates who attended the rather more civilised bouts in later years, he represented a focal point for skill, competition and endeavour.

There would be other boxers, bigger and possibly better, but the world of sport was surely a poorer place for Fitzsimmons s absence. Rocky Marciano would thrill audiences with his pound-for-pound strength, Muhammad Ali would astonish the world with an uncanny agility; but both men owed a large debt to Fitzsimmons and his ilk, who transformed boxing from street scrap to spectator sport. As Fitzsimmons, Corbett and Sullivan grew into old age, their names would become romantically linked with an era of prizefighting which was like no other. An era that would never be repeated. Today, they are revered as founding fathers, ground-breaking pioneers, swash-buckling gladiators. They will be forever remembered as the men who used their fists to earn a dirty, dangerous living; surviving pain, scarring and disfigurement in marathon contests which only ended when one of the protagonists went down and stayed down.

And now, fading pictures show a collection of burly, tough-looking young men, incongruously attired in boots and tights, with decorative scarves tied around their waists. Their classic poses, with clenched bare-knuckles held out before them, show them in their prime; willing and able to take on another man in a test of strength, skill and endurance which we, in our cosseted, pampered society, can scarcely begin to imagine. They *were* the prizefighters. And they will forever remain prizefighters.

As a man reaches a certain age, he begins more and more to look to his offspring — a new age of hope, who will carry the family name on into the future. In the case of a father and son, the former may look to the latter to continue the particular furrow that he himself has been ploughing; that is, to match his achievements, and, if possible, go on to better them. It is in this fashion that the ancestral baton is passed from generation to generation.

PRIZE FIGHTER

So it appeared to be, in the case of Robert Fitzsimmons, who had achieved more in his colourful life than almost any man would even dare dream of. The former champion was in a philosophical mood when talking to one particular newspaperman. Opening his heart in his usual feet-first fashion, he told the journalist that he had a hope for the future; a proud hope that all he d accomplished would eventually be eclipsed by the heroic deeds of his own son, Robert Junior. He claimed the young man was showing an astounding potential, far greater than he himself had shown at the same age. He excitedly boasted that the boy would one day reclaim his father s world heavyweight title — putting the name of Fitzsimmons into the history books for the second time. He told the reporter:

> My boy, Bobby, is the coming heavyweight champion of the world. Not only that, but he s going to be the greatest champion we ever had. It may sound queer to people who don t know him, but I m willing to match him against Jack Johnson or Gunboat Smith (another heavyweight contender of the time). I d bet every nickel I have that neither one of them could lay a glove on him in four rounds.
>
> I know that no previous champion has ever reached the top without a lot of experience and a number of hard fights. Well, this one will be the exception. Jeffries didn t have many fights before he was champion, and my boy is going to be bigger and more powerful than Jeffries, and twice as fast as Corbett, and he s going to know all I know about fighting.

In addition, he went so far as to say that Fitzsimmons the Younger was stronger, faster, fitter and braver than he himself had ever been. This would have been a truly exciting prospect for followers of the fighting art, and Bob Senior knew it. In bragging of his son s abilities and comparing them favourably to his own, he may have imagined he was providing a launchpad from which world domination would surely be one step away. After all, it s not every up-and-coming fighter who s personally recommended by a former world champion, even if they do happen to share the same surname. Any claims of parental bias, however, were dismissed out of hand by the enthusiastic father, as he continued to extol his son s many virtues: Why, he was bred to be a champion. His mother was the greatest acrobat that ever lived and some people think I was the greatest fighter. If there s anything in heredity, he ought to have all our best points. And he has. He has my fighting instinct and his mother s gracefulness and round muscles and strength. I never wanted him to be a fighter and I never taught him how to fight. One day a couple of years ago, I heard that he had fought a big ironworker who had been knocking out a lot of men in short time. Bobby closed his eyes and beat him up at a little club down in Jersey, until they stopped the bout.

Regarding the incident to which he refers, Bob Junior certainly seemed destined to live up to this kudos when, in September 1912, at the age of sixteen, he knocked out Kid Harris within the first round of their meeting in his home town of Dunellen, New Jersey. If further fuel were needed, this early success seems to have stoked his father s ambitions still further. He boasted: He will lick all the fighters in the world, black or white, and do it so quickly you won t have time to turn around and expectorate. And so far as skill and cleverness goes, Jim Corbett in his palmiest days would look like a truck horse in comparison. And as for strength and punching power, Young Bob has Jeffries tied in a knot even when the big boiler-maker was the real thing . . . I m not bragging about my boy without cause, because I have tried him out a number of times, and found *I* am a mere child in his hands.

As usual, Bob s carefully thought out strategy didn t quite go according to plan. In effect, he was actually creating a huge weight to hang on his son s shoulders, one which would prove impossible to shake off. Any comparison with one of the greatest fighters in history turned out to be both unjustified and unfair. A bizarre exhibition bout took place on 27 March 1916 in Troy, New Jersey, which saw father and son putting on the gloves and squaring up in the ring. Some correspondents have reported that this was part of a series of non-competitive showcases, designed to exhibit the boy s talent, while replenishing the family purse and also giving the old man some exercise. But when he took on opponents to whom he wasn t related, Fitzsimmons Junior failed to re-ignite the family flame which had formerly burned with such brightness.

Beyond mere parental pride, Bob Senior s words carried a secret burden — that of loading all his unfulfilled dreams and ambitions on the boy s shoulders, so he could achieve even those things which his father hadn t. Clearly longing for his own glory days, the old man was trying to live those times again, albeit vicariously, through his son and heir. It says less about the son s actual prowess than about the Cornishman s continued hunger for success. In referring to the likes of Corbett and Jeffries, the old man was clearly trying to exorcise ghosts from his own past and he would have dearly liked to get in the ring again with either of these characters for a good tear-up. Perhaps subconsciously, his insistence that his son would far outweigh these old stagers is indicative that he still harboured desires to see those men beaten. Boxing historians report that young Bob fought several times at competitive level, but he didn t make any kind of impression on the sport which his father had once held in the palm of his hand. He fought a number of bouts between 1919 and 1931. While he was never knocked out or stopped, his opponents didn t crumple before him as they had before Fitzsimmons Senior.

One unconfirmed report, contained in the compilation of essays from the Cornish Women s Institute, has it that there was another, darker, reason why Young Bob s career came to an end. This was due to the death of his last opponent following their fight — a shattering experience for any professional boxer, and one which had twice befallen Fitzsimmons Senior. Whether or not this was the case, it certainly seems clear that the young Fitzsimmons did not possess the same appetite for the sport that had consumed his father so entirely, if indeed he could not face stepping back into the ring having caused the death of another man.

So, at the age of thirty-five, Young Bob Fitzsimmons was forced to admit defeat in his impossible quest to emulate the inimitable, and he retired from the ring for good. In the preceding years, those who d been watching in anticipation of a flash of the old man s legendary speed and skill would have been disappointed. For boxing fans, there would only ever be one Robert Fitzsimmons.

While his own lineage would peter out in terms of boxing glory, there were many others who would be inspired by the feats of Fitzsimmons as the sport exploded in popularity during the early part of the twentieth century. The men who would descend from that first generation of professional prize fighters would go on to capture the public s imagination in the same way, while those aforementioned greying veterans retired to their country estates or suburban mansions, usually maintaining that the standard of current fighters was infinitely inferior to that of their day. For his part, Fitzsimmons himself resolutely believed to the end of his career that he was still capable of taking on the biggest and best heavyweights to appear on the scene. This was in the face of all sensible opinion, and despite the fact that one of them, Jack Johnson, had effortlessly meted out a fearful thrashing in their hopelessly one-sided contest. One particular member of this emerging new breed of supermen is particularly worthy of mention in the same breath as his legendary predecessors, as he gained enormously from their growing appeal at the box office. In the world title fight of 1919, one of the names heading the bill had a very familiar ring to it.

William Harrison Dempsey was born in Manassa, Colorado, on 24 June 1895. Fitzsimmons was still two years away from gaining the heavyweight crown at this time, and gloved fighting was still in its relative infancy. It s significant that in later years, young William chose one of those aforementioned old-time heroes as an inspiration for his own professional career, re-christening himself Jack Dempsey. The model of his ambitions was none other than the great Nonpareil — the middleweight champion whom Fitzsimmons had beaten so dramatically soon after arriving on American shores.

Of course, in paying this ultimate mark of respect, the two would forever be confused as being one and the same person, although it was Dempsey Mark Two who would actually go on to enjoy the greater success.

Often referred to as the Manassa Mauler , or simply The Idol , Dempsey was a tough young man, who combined Corbett s tactical awareness with Fitzsimmons s iron fists. Standing six feet one tall and weighing in at around 180 pounds, he served his fighting apprenticeship in the so-called tank towns across Colorado, Utah and Nevada. He graduated from the backstreet circuit when he met a man named Jack Kearns in a San Francisco bar in 1917. Kearns would transform the young prizefighter into a world-class contender, catapulting him into a new world of money, titles and more money. With the backing of legendary promoter Tex Rickard, Dempsey soon became the most marketable commodity boxing had ever seen, with a worldwide following not seen since the days of John L Sullivan.

Our story again becomes intertwined when Dempsey s opponent was announced for the title fight — the outsized former cowboy, Jess Willard. The date set for the fight was 4 July 1919. It had been Willard who had cut short the title reign of Jack Johnson, who in turn had humiliatingly hastened Fitzsimmons s retirement. The bout between Dempsey and Willard would go down in boxing history as one of the most merciless beatings ever inflicted within the ropes. Six feet six inches tall and scaling over 250 pounds, Willard was nevertheless powerless to stem the unbridled aggression of the twenty-four-year-old challenger. The bout, which was staged in Toledo, Ohio, lasted only three rounds. Willard dropped to the canvas no fewer than seven times in the first of these, each time gingerly picking himself up to take another caning. The vulnerable champion was battered semi-conscious, with blood flowing freely from his mouth and nose, and his eyes staring glassily in their daze.

By the end of the second round, he d lost two of his front teeth, his face was swollen beyond all recognition and his right eye was closed. Still he fought on, hoping against hope for an opening like the one which had dispatched Johnson to the floor before him four years before. Although he s since been rated as one of the poorest heavyweight champions, partly due to his reputed distaste for heavy training, Willard showed his real mettle in soaking up the relentless physical abuse being dished out by the rampant Dempsey. The fight was finally stopped after the third round, when Big Jess called the referee over to his corner, and promptly announced his retirement. Dempsey was crowned champion, and the latest monarch s reign had already begun.

IN RETIREMENT

By coincidence, yet another character from our story also had a significant role to play in the Dempsey—Willard fight. One of those trusted with the unenviable task of knocking the reluctant Willard into shape in his training camp was one James Jeffries, the man who d himself been stopped by Johnson. Now aged forty-four, the former professional used his hard-won expertise to attempt to coax a winning performance out of the sluggish, workshy heavyweight. On witnessing his prot g s dismal performance, fight fans may have wished that the heavyset ex-champ — still boasting the husky build of a professional fighter — had come out of retirement and stepped through the ropes to face Dempsey himself.

17. Money Problems

Unbelievable as it seems, by the time he was finally forced into hanging up his gloves for good, Fitzsimmons was virtually penniless. The man who d once rubbed exquisitely tailored shoulders with presidents and showbiz megastars was well and truly broke. It seemed the years of high-living and expensive wives had taken its toll on the sizeable fortune amassed by his appearances in the ring and on the stage. To this day, it s still unclear exactly how his finances came to be in such a parlous state, as he once received around $40,000 for a single fight during the lucrative peak of his career. It was actually Fitzsimmons himself who made this story public, so caution is advised before treating it as absolute gospel. Nevertheless, if the claim is true, this sum would have been a veritable fortune in the 1890s, worth the equivalent of more than twenty million pounds in today s money, which should certainly have seen him and his family well into comfortable retirement. In real terms, he actually earned more than modern-day boxers, with fifteen million dollars currently being regarded as the likely purse of a crowd-pulling world heavyweight champion.

Taking the Carson City title bout as an example, the betting dividends and appearance fee, combined with the winner s purse, gave him an evening s pay cheque of $25,000 in an age when most people would be lucky to earn a few dollars per week. This can be put into context, however, when compared with the expenses claimed by promoter Dan Stuart for staging the event, which totalled over one million dollars. According to financial records, this included the construction of the arena, the provision of telegraphic poles for newspapermen to send telegrams and transport of sufficient luxury to bring the two fighters to the venue. Extra transport was also needed to ferry around many of the spectators, as Carson s infrastructure wasn t yet sufficiently developed to accommodate this immense influx of people. For the honour of witnessing in person the much-vaunted duel between Fitzsimmons and Corbett, the 8,000 fans lucky enough to obtain tickets were asked to pay the princely sum of $20, while many more bills would have changed hands during the course of on-site betting. Incidentally, the odds were firmly against the Cornishman, who ranked as a 6-10 outsider on the morning of the fight. Closer examination of these financial records illustrate the size and scale of the project — equivalent to building a brand-new five-star hotel today. The telegraph poles alone cost almost half a million dollars to erect and equip, while Stuart s personal expenses topped the twenty-thousand-dollar mark.

A clue to Fitzsimmons s eventual predicament can perhaps be traced in an explanation he once gave for taking on a fight when he wasn t physically prepared for it. I just needed the money, he explained rather sheepishly, adding that he had recently lost a lot of cash in ill-advised stock market investments. During the course of Fitzsimmons s life, a true rags-to-riches-then-back-to-rags tale can be traced. Although his father s wages as a policeman would have been better than those of the majority of his impoverished fellow countrymen, the strain placed by twelve children on the family finances would have meant that the Fitzsimmons family were far from wealthy. As the youngest of twelve, Robert had to attire himself in the hand-me-downs of his elder brothers. So although the family weren t forced to endure the grinding poverty of many working-class communities in England at that time, there would have been scarcely enough for anything beyond basic necessities.

It was when he discovered his true God-given talent that he really found himself, as he put it, on the road to Easy Street . Even at the start of his fledgling career, he could earn more in a few violent, bone-cracking minutes in the dirt square than in a month of back-breaking endeavour at the forge. On winning his first bare-knuckle prize fights at the age of fifteen, this would have become all too apparent to the young blacksmith. With a few flashes of his bony fists, he could support himself for weeks to come. At the height of his earning capacity, we re told by all who knew him that Bob liked to live life high on the hog, wallowing in his new-found wealth, and extensively stocking the family home in New York with all manner of food and drink, in order to entertain the couple s many friends. The Bath Beach home he shared with Rose and their children during the 1890s became known in New York social circles for lavish hospitality and good living. But while Fitz brought the money in, it was his rather more shrewd wife who controlled the purse strings. While her husband tended to experience glorious fits of outrageous extravagance, his wife was solely responsible for reining in those excesses, while taking care to ensure all the bills were paid. When Rose died, it was discovered that the deeds of the house were in her name. She had left it to their children in her will; to be inherited when they reached adulthood. While this ensured a nest-egg for their offspring, it left the master of the house somewhat embarrassingly bereft of material assets. He was quick to apportion the blame for this sorry state of affairs. In a letter to the *Mirror of Life* newspaper in Britain, Fitzsimmons claimed: I wish to make a statement to the public that during my career I have been robbed of more than $100,000 in purses and managerial shares. From the moment I arrived in this country from Australia, I have certainly been up against a stiff game, for when I wasn t swindled out of purses I fought for, I was being robbed of the money I was entitled to by the different sleek managers I had looking after my business interests. He continued: I realise now how easily I was euchred out of my money, for I was such an easy-going fellow that everyone took advantage of me. Fight promoters and managers gave me whatever money they felt like, and pocketed the rest. Almost certainly referring to his brother-in-law, among others, he added: I had the misfortune to be swindled by my manager. I don t care about stating who my managers were, for although they robbed me right and left at every chance they got, I don t care about letting the public speak harshly of them. After figuring up my losses, I can safely say, without fear of contradiction, that I have been swindled out of $125,000. In the matter of purses I lost $80,000, and my managers got the rest.

While early fights in New Zealand and Australia would hardly have amounted to a living wage, the sort of sums he could demand rose sharply after the shock win over Jack Dempsey, when he claimed the middleweight title. In addition to the winning prizes, there were fringe benefits, such as the $10,000 deal signed with the *New York Journal* prior to the Corbett title bout which guaranteed exclusive rights to the boxer s many words of wisdom as they poured forth, before and after the fight. To sign up a loose cannon like Fitzsimmons, who was likely to say anything about anybody, regardless of the consequences, must have seemed to the newspaper editor concerned to be money well spent. The arrangement was an early forerunner of today s million-dollar deals, when celebrities sell the rights of their various stories to glossy magazines. Such was Fitz s apparent enthusiasm for seeing his name in print, however, it s likely he would have actually paid the paper for the privilege.

But it was his exploits *in* the ring at this time which would continue to reap sizeable benefits. He narrowly missed out on a $10,000 pay cheque from the 1896 fight with Tom Sharkey, thanks to Wyatt Earp s untimely interference. But it was on beating Corbett for the world heavyweight title that his financial boat really came in. The icing on the cake would have been the lucrative stage appearances garnered by his reputation. These are difficult to calculate, as his fees would have varied widely, but John Sullivan was said to have received a total of more than $900,000 from theatre appearances during his career, so we can assume Fitz wasn t selling himself short in this endeavour either. The fact that he dispensed with managers and agents completely for his last few fights tells its own story, as he continued to complain bitterly that if he had followed this course from the start of his career, he d have been a rich man until the day he died.

As it was, the sum total of his possessions at the time of his death were eight diamond fillings which he d had inserted in his teeth in typically understated style during his days of *largesse*, and a pair of diamond cuff-links. Jewellery seemed to hold a special fascination for the former blacksmith, perhaps due to his having worked with metals for much of his early life. Certainly, he seemed irresistibly drawn to valuable trinkets, as if mesmerised by the glare of the shiny stones which symbolise money and success. He claimed to have spent hundreds of thousands of pounds on jewellery for his third wife, Julia May Gifford, while his fourth wife was also said to have been left with around $150,000 worth of precious baubles.

But at the very end, he was left with nothing. Even the costs of his grave and funeral had to be met by the American Board of Boxing Control, while his headstone was provided free of charge by a stonemasons association. Having entered life back in Cornwall with practically nothing to his name, Bob Fitzsimmons would leave it in exactly the same way.

The quiet, dignified atmosphere of the courtroom was in sharp contrast to the deeply undignified episode which was currently being related within its austere, oak-panelled walls. Whereas accounts of Bob Fitzsimmons s fistic exploits had once been breathlessly recounted in verbal technicolour on the sports pages of newspapers across the world, this latest report of his indubitable physical prowess was being rather more soberly outlined by a prosecution lawyer.

Appearing before a criminal court, having been arrested and charged with assault, Fitzsimmons apparently showed little of the remorse which may have been expected, considering his latest indiscretion. The fact that a three-times former world boxing champion was in the dock, having assaulted a creditor who was attempting to repossess his home, spoke volumes about the general direction in which Fitzsimmons s life appeared to be heading. The only saving grace appeared to be that the hapless victim hadn t suffered a more serious injury at the hands of his assailant, which was all the more fortunate considering the latter s legendary skill with his fists. The case originally arose from a number of sizeable debts which had been accrued by Bob during the course of his ambitious efforts to convert his New Jersey farm into a health resort. While the progress of these plans remained uncharted, the bills remained unpaid. This sorry impasse served as further proof that Fitz was now facing severe financial hardship, as his earning capacity went into a dramatic tailspin. It seemed as if all those ill-advised deals and acts of spontaneous generosity during his better days had now come back to haunt him.

According to New Jersey local records one gentleman who maintained a close personal interest in the resort scheme was a Mr J Hendricks from Atlantic City. Mr Hendricks said he d loaned money to Fitz, on the strength of his plans, but had received neither profit nor repayment on his investment. Having first secured an eviction notice on the farm in order to recover the undisclosed sum, he then turned up to see Fitzsimmons off the premises. To the more cautious of us, the wisdom of this boldly direct approach may have seemed, at best, questionable. Exactly what happened next isn t quite clear, due to wildly conflicting reports from those involved. It almost goes without saying that Bob was naturally less than thrilled to see his former business partner under these circumstances, whereupon a fight apparently ensued. Somewhat predictably, Hendricks came off worse in this particular contest, and subsequently pressed charges of assault, which duly led to the Cornishman s appearance in a New Jersey court. If the seriousness of this latest predicament — namely, being hauled before a judge — was apparent to Bob, he was characteristically nonchalant about the whole messy affair. Somewhat surprisingly, at least for those who didn t know him, Fitzsimmons even appeared to be enjoying this brief return to a public arena. When asked by the court to justify his actions in striking Mr Hendricks, Fitz did so vehemently, insisting with great gusto that the other man had struck him first. To the amusement of those present, the former world heavyweight champion then enthusiastically re-enacted this most recent exhibition of his most famous talent. As part of his defence, he claimed: He bashed me on the jaw; then bing, bing, bing, my good left went out, first in the face and then in the solar plexus. It was the same old punch I used on Jim Corbett, and the one that enabled me to be the best in the world.

No doubt the public gallery was enjoying the colourful blow-by-blow account as related by the practised raconteur, but from a defence point of view, it was immediately clear that Bob wasn t cut out for a career in the legal profession. Somewhat alarmingly in view of his advancing age, the ex-boxer then added wistfully:

Maybe I shall get the chance to use it on someone else. Quick with the counterpunch, the judge presiding over the case asked: I trust you do not mean anyone in this court? Never willing to be out-pointed, Fitzsimmons replied: It could be Jess Willard. This was greeted with hoots of derision from the benches, for the Kansan who d recently claimed Fitzsimmons s former crown was regarded as one of the largest men ever to enter a ring, and the thought of the elderly Cornishman coming out of retirement to take him on was considered highly comical. Whether or not he was a boxing fan, the judge must certainly have appreciated Bob s sense of humour, as the unrepenting defendant was fined $10 and placed on probation for twelve months.

To outsiders, he would have appeared to be the Bob of old; full of wise-cracking belligerence. The reality, though, was rather different. Although he d revelled in his fleeting moment of newfound fame, the indignity of the episode characterised his life at the time, as things steadily went from bad to worse. His competitive career was over, but his high-maintenance lifestyle meant he simply couldn t afford to retire. While there s only one heavyweight champion (or at least there was at that time), there are any number of ex-champions who are forced to find other ways in which to make a living when their fighting days are done. It s a scenario which was repeated countless times throughout the following century, as world-beating fighters have been divested of their transient fortunes by the taxman, the divorce lawyers, or both.

Bob had found solace of sorts on the variety stage, where he could act out his showman fantasies, and he even enjoyed some success in this field. But he missed the adrenaline rush of the prizefighting ring, the air of physical competition which had, for so long, been such an integral part of his very being. More than the money, more than the glamour, he discovered a large vacuum in his day-to-day existence, which had formerly been filled with fights, plans for fights, preparations for fights, interviews about fights and so on and so on.

As in all fields, the old veteran remained convinced that it was his generation who d set the standard, with the new blood singularly failing to live up to it. Interviews and comments from this time show him resolute in his belief that if he was given the chance to once again pull on the gloves he could wipe the floor with the young upstarts who were currently ruling the roost. They would soon find out, he claimed, that experience counted over youth, adding that his skills were as polished now as when he d faced the likes of Corbett and Jeffries back in the last century. But of course that would never happen. No-one was likely to take any notice of a bitter ex-fighter, who claimed against popular opinion that he still had one or two good fights left in him. He could only re-live the glory days in his head, as he waited to take the stage in his latest play or cameo appearance. And he would have needed to play to an awful lot of packed houses to rediscover the sheer adulation to which he d once been accustomed.

Retirement can be looked upon as a long-awaited pleasure, a welcome light at the end of the long tunnel of work. Many people who leave the tumultuous worlds of commerce or industry find new pleasures in tending their gardens, spending time with their families, or simply pausing to take stock.

Those people who expected Bob Fitzsimmons to pursue a somewhat less riotous life in his twilight years would clearly have been backing entirely the wrong horse. Rather than mellowing in his old age, he appeared to be gaining momentum. Seemingly without pausing for breath, after the personal and professional upheavals of recent years, he came back fighting on all fronts. Firstly, he met and married his fourth wife, amid his usual whirlwind of emotions. Once again, Cupid s arrow appeared to have hit the ageing ex-pro, as his life was once again overtaken by an all-consuming passion which he was apparently powerless to resist. The lucky object of these lavish affections was thirty-two-year-old divorc e Temo Slomonin, lately of Portland, Oregon.

There are many fascinating stories surrounding the latest of Bob s wives and once again they veer wildly between believable fact and fanciful fiction. One legend relates that the former prizefighter met the young woman while she was still a teenager in her homeland of Russia. Quite what Fitz was doing in Russia is anybody s guess, but in any case, that particular aspect of the story isn t recorded. The tale has it that the international celebrity befriended the young singer (she apparently appeared in various light opera performances) and eventually rescued her and her entire family from anti-Semitic persecution, arranging for them all to be transported to begin a new life in the United States. The source of this isn t known, but it does have a very dramatic ring to it, in which case it almost certainly emanated from Fitzsimmons himself. While this would cast grave doubts as to its authenticity, that s not to say that there isn t more than a grain of truth in it, for it s just the sort of impulsive, sweeping gesture he would have afforded anyone who d won his affection. Other reports simply say that he met the Russian immigrant while visiting the city of Chicago, whereupon they immediately fell in love. Regardless of the circumstances, when they later became man and wife, proclaiming their unequivocal and undying love for each other, they immediately embarked on Bob s traditional choice of honeymoon — a boxing match. At least this one did involve some foreign travel for his newest bride; they journeyed to the Jack Johnson—Jess Willard fight down in Havana, where they watched Johnson counted out in the glare of the Cuban sunshine, as Willard knocked the Galveston Giant to the canvas.

Like her predecessor, Temo may have had some misgivings about sharing the man to whom she d so recently pledged her troth with the many thousands of fight followers who also flocked to the big event, but it s likely that Bob s enthusiasm would have brushed such qualms aside. Friends and colleagues of the ex-boxer may have expressed concerns over the seemingly reckless speed at which Bob seemed to be collecting wives in recent years; but for the time being, the couple seemed as happy as could be expected, settling in together at the Dunellen farm. Fitz had become something of a pet local celebrity within the New Jersey town since buying the property near what is now Warrenville Rd, just outside the Dunellen border. Although his fighting days were long past now, he remained a colourful character who was popular among the local residents, who would point him out to others when he was jogging through the town, or simply passing the time of day with acquaintances. He even went so far as to join the Dunellen Field

Club, being elected to the post of vice-president in August 1909. Local records state that: Lanky Bob was elected to the office after having signified his willingness to help the club out by allowing the use of his name. It was thought that the presence of Fitz on the board of officers would give added prestige to the club. It seemed the one-time illegal prizefighter had indeed become a veritable pillar of the community.

If the community welcomed the ex-pugilist and his family into their fold, however, there was one rather less popular member of his household who remained strictly persona non grata, especially among tradesmen and visitors. This was Senator, his pet lion, a throwback to the days when lion-wrestling formed a vital part of the Fitzsimmons training routine, albeit more for reasons of showmanship than exercise. Senator was tethered to a heavy wire, in order that he should have enough room to stretch his mighty legs, although those passing by apparently harboured serious misgivings about their safety. These fears were confirmed on more than one occasion, when the huge animal broke free of its moorings and roamed free across the property. One of these incidents occurred just as a man named William Gallagher had the misfortune to be driving a carriage into the yard. Senator tore away from his restraints and leapt upon one of Mr Gallagher s horses. Landing heavily on top of the stricken beast, it sank its teeth into its neck, while its owner could only watch, horrified. Amidst the pandemonium, the master of the house appeared from within, and never being one to stand idly by in any kind of conflict, immediately launched himself at his errant pet. Realising he wasn t capable of overpowering the lion, Fitz looked around for a handy weapon and happened upon a large hammer. He then proceeded to batter the unrepentant Senator about the head with this until the animal fell, unconscious, at his feet. Surprisingly, the horse wasn t as badly hurt as had been thought, and Fitzsimmons completed his day s work by using his experience in the trade to sew up the wound, deftly administering twelve neat stitches.

Apart from their unsociable pets, the newly-weds were described as being charming company. One gentleman who enjoyed the pleasure of this company was one Sir Robert Lockheart, who invited the couple to dinner at his house in Vancouver, while Temo was appearing in the city. He reported an enchanting evening of food, drink and conversation, all of a pleasingly high standard. He described the ex-boxer as unspoiled , relating how he spoke dispassionately about his various triumphs, along with those of other people. Along with such social niceties, the newly-wed couple were about to discover a common purpose which would unite them beyond their marriage. With Alice, his first wife, Fitz had embarked on a joint adventure in emigrating to Australia and launching his professional career. With Rose, he had shared a driving ambition to climb to the very summit of his chosen calling. With Julia, he had enjoyed a common passion for the theatre. Subsequently with Temo, it was in another field entirely that Bob would join forces, and it was one which would dominate the rest of his life, opening up a whole new chapter in his larger-than-life story.

The path of Bob s fortunes was never destined to run smoothly, and, true to form, he was still walking a high-wire between triumph and disaster during the latter part of 1915. He and Temo had split up only months after the blessing of their union — an acrimonious parting which wasn t helped at all by her obtaining a court judgement against him for the debt of $1,000. This came at a time of ever more acute financial cramp for the perpetually cash-strapped Fitz. His household effects had had to be auctioned off to repay his creditors. Having already delayed the repossession of his home, it was finally sold off by the sheriff s office, having been instituted by the divorce settlement to Julia. It fetched only one hundred dollars. Even his Sterns automobile — a highly-prized possession in those early days of motorised travel — had to be sold off by a local garage-owner, Gus Barfus, because his bill hadn t been paid. Fitz overcame these hardships and even became reunited with Temo the following year, despite their earlier financial dispute. It was following this reconciliation that Bob embarked on his fourth career. From blacksmith to boxer, to theatre performer and now . . . evangelist.

Temo had found religion in a big way during their time apart, and she had gone on the road in pursuit of this ideal, travelling across the country, preaching the gospel. Naturally, Fitzsimmons now embraced this with a zeal which would have converted the entire United States of America, should they be fortunate enough to be granted an audience with him. His wife would say later that he was even planning to attend the famous Moody Bible Institute in Chicago, in order that he be fully prepared for the long and rocky road to salvation that lay ahead. The Institute was named after its founder, Dwight L Moody, a former travelling salesman who was famed for his lectern-thumping sermons in which he urged the world to save itself from damnation. Interestingly, there are several parallels to be drawn between the famous preacher and the famous ex-boxer, although it s unlikely they ever met, as Moody died in 1899, some years before Fitzsimmons found religion.

Turning his back on a successful career in business, Moody had thrown himself into the activities of the Church, establishing the undenominational Illinois Street Church and travelling to national Sunday School conventions. In 1873 he toured the British Isles, where he became a national figure and millions of people flocked to his meetings. He later became one of the best-known preachers in the world, with his passion and commitment endearing him to those who witnessed his colourful appearances. It was in 1886 that he started the Chicago Evangelisation Society, which later became the Moody Bible Institute. Like Fitzsimmons, he d left his indelible mark on the field he d dominated.

It s likely that the newly converted Fitzsimmons would have attended at least one of the rallies held during the early part of 1917 in Chicago, where, in a Billy Graham-style address, the speakers would renounce sin in all its forms and call for their brothers and sisters to take up the battle alongside them. In attracting one of the most high-profile celebrities of the age, the Institute would have achieved a major coup in publicity terms, especially as this potential recruit was, in his former life, a common pugilist. If ever there were a group of people in need of a spot of redeeming, the boxing world was surely it. (Coincidentally, another former exponent of the bare-knuckled art had also taken to the pulpit by this time. The notorious John L Sullivan — he of the one-time fearsome temper and raging bare-knuckle brawls — was appearing at venues around the country in the role of Temperance preacher, warning the public of the demons which could be found at the bottom of a bottle.) So, committed to doing God s work and battling evil in all forms, Mr and Mrs Fitzsimmons toured halls and theatres across the States, spreading fire and brimstone in their wake.

It was something of a departure from his musical efforts as the Singing Blacksmith and an even more radical turn from his prizefighting days, but we must assume that the Cornishman approached this latest mission with much the same reckless abandon as his previous endeavours. We must assume as a coincidence the fact that he chose this period of his life to become closer to God. He can t have known that as the year of 1917 dawned, his time was fast running out . . .

18. Final Curtain Call

For Mr Arthur Sobey, of Butte City, Montana, it was one of the most exciting days of his life. One of his all-time heroes, the great fighter Bob Fitzsimmons, was visiting his humble blacksmith s, having taken part in an exhibition match nearby in the town with his son, Bob Junior. The occasion was a pleasurable one for the great man too, for it was here at Mr Sobey s forge that he met a number of his fellow countrymen, in the form of a group of Cornish immigrants who lived in the area. Clearly relaxed in their company, Fitzsimmons chatted with them about the native county they shared, no doubt commenting on the undeniable quality of people who hailed from that particular corner of the British Isles. Fitz treated those present at the blacksmith s to an impromptu display of his former trade, fashioning a horse-shoe with a speed and deftness that showed he d lost little of his former skill. Finishing with a flourish, he engraved the shoe with his name and presented it to Mr Sobey as a keepsake of the day, all the while laughing and joking with his new-found friends. Traditionally signifying good luck, the piece of metal was proudly displayed at the shop from that day on. However, it wasn t to bring any good luck to Fitzsimmons himself. Neither he nor his companions that day knew at that time that the ex-boxer had less than three months to live.

For the maestro, the final bow came in the early hours of 22 October 1917. For someone whose life had been one long performance, the curtain fell suddenly, and without warning. Robert James Fitzsimmons died at the Michael Reese Hospital in Chicago of lobar pneumonia. He was fifty-four years old.

PRIZE FIGHTER

It s perhaps ironic that at a time when he had — at long last — finally begun to ease back from the frantic pace which had driven him until then, his life was suddenly taken from him. It s even a possibility that it was this very sudden change in lifestyle which may have contributed to his illness, as his once-potent life-force began to gradually ebb away. The man who d been begged and cajoled by his friends and family to give up the bruising, highly dangerous living for which he d grown far too old, had instead been struck down by a silent, creeping assassin. The former champion, who d overcome fractures, concussion and serious wounding from his peers had finally taken on one opponent too many. That opponent was his own failing health.

Temo was left widowed, devastated at the loss of the man with whom she d shared such a tumultuous relationship. She told everyone that it was Bob s wish that she should throw herself even more whole-heartedly into her religious endeavours, continuing the fight against evil with the same vigour that her late husband had employed in the boxing ring.

Meanwhile, across the globe, the entire sporting world was immediately pitched into mourning for one of the most colourful characters who would ever grace any public arena, anywhere. Arguably the greatest fighter the world had ever produced had died and part of the art which he d made famous had surely died with him. The *New York Times* used a large banner headline to mark his passing, stating that the famous champion had passed away after a brief illness. It described him as being a fighter by inheritance . It recounted his early prizefighting days in New Zealand and Australia, where he was fondly known as Lanky Bob , and reports on the suspicion which surrounded him when he first arrived on American shores, having apparently taken a dive against Jim Hall. The obituary incorrectly states the year of his birth as being 1862, although this was a common mistake as Fitzsimmons himself was never actually sure. In fact, his official birth certificate from local records in Cornwall shows he came into the world in the year 1863. The obituary continues to describe him as being as supple and strong as any fighter in the ring , quoting a phrase from an unknown source which amusingly likened his unorthodox frame to a cannonball on a pair of pipe stems . Also relating his brushes with authority, the paper recalls how the police broke up an 1894 bout with Joe Choynski, just as Choynski was on the verge of receiving a severe beating.

Back in his native Cornwall, a local newspaper paid its own tribute to one of the county s most famous sons. It painted a picture of a man who was tall, lean, big-boned and immensely strong . It repeated the observation that Fitz s bearing was rather different from many of his behemoth counterparts, although his larger-than-life public image did much to dwarf his opponents in and out of the ring. There never was a more tenacious puncher, nor one with a more terrible punch, commented the writer.

Over in America, among those who sent wreaths and messages of condolence to the Fitzsimmons family was John Sullivan. At war during their ring careers, and still in disagreement at the end of their days, the former Boston Strong Boy was nevertheless quick to mark the departure of his sporting colleague with words of comfort for those Bob had left behind.

It served as a reminder of the immense popularity in which Fitzsimmons had basked, while also showing just how many people were personally affected by his death. It s likely the man himself would have approved of this high-profile exit, with its tributes and headlines. It would possibly have compensated for losing his final fight, the battle against his own mortality. As he once said: I was ever a fighter — so one fight more — the best and the last . . .

It was a scene akin to a state funeral or national day of remembrance. Flowers, cards, words of sorrow, messages of sympathy. More than three thousand mourners, dressed in doleful black, crowded into Chicago s Moody Tabernacle to mark the passing of their friend, their colleague, their hero. Just as he drew huge crowds in his glory days, Robert James Fitzsimmons was well attended one last time, as those who knew him turned out to say goodbye. It was a final performance which would do justice to the legend which had been created around the man himself. A reminder of the dire financial straits in which Bob had latterly found himself could be noted by the fact that the service was paid for by the American boxing authorities, as the Fitzsimmons estate couldn t afford it. A bronze plinth was also respectfully donated as a parting gift.

The *New York Times* of 25 October 1917 records the event in its pages, describing the departed as a former champion heavyweight pugilist . It also says that the clergyman conducting the service, a Reverend Paul Rader, had connections to the sporting world himself, as a former Pacific Coast college athlete.

In death, as in life, Bob wasn t without controversy. His widow Temo was the only member of his family present at the burial, following a dispute with Bob Junior. He d come to Chicago following his father s death, but had left before the ceremony, returning to his job as an Army boxing instructor. His siblings apparently stayed away in solidarity with him, showing their apparent disapproval of their father s fourth wife. It s likely that resentment with his passing which had been bubbling away since the marriage had finally come to the boil.

One of the most poignant features of the funeral service itself was a written message which had been sent by none other than James Corbett — the man who d stood toe-to-toe with Fitzsimmons in a battle for supremacy which characterised the boxing era that they both dominated. Bitter rivals, arch-enemies, polar opposites — the two had scuffled, quarrelled and jostled several times in public before they finally got to meet in that Carson City prize ring on St Patrick s Day, 1897.

Following Bob s death, Temo would go on to embark on two more marriages, both of which would also end in widowhood. She wrote a book about her life with the boxing legend and tried unsuccessfully to sell the rights to a Hollywood motion picture studio. She intended to use the money for the charitable causes with which she was heavily involved, in accordance with Bob s last wishes. In the four years following Fitz s death, she went through every last penny she d received during their time together, including $150,000 worth of jewellery and ninety-one acres of freehold land in upstate New York. She used it all to support her work with the needy, which she later continued by joining the

Salvation Army, to work across Europe. During her old age in the late 1950s, she is known to have resided at a home for Christian Hebrews down in Tampa, Florida. She died in a Los Angeles hospital in 1959, having suffered a stroke.

The Fitzsimmons family line continued in New Zealand, America and Cornwall. In Timaru, Bob s brother Jarrett was succeeded by his children and grandchildren. Back in Cornwall, there was the Mitchell family of Mawgan, whose grandmother had been Fitz s first cousin. They are said to have shared a striking resemblance to their famous relative, with freckled faces and red hair. Meanwhile in the States, Jean and Joy Fitzsimmons — Bob s grandchildren through his son, Bob Junior — achieved their own fame when they became nationally-rated swimming champions following contests in New Jersey and Florida. They became renowned during the 50s for their water ballet displays at Miami Beach, where they entertained sizeable crowds. They almost certainly inherited this showmanship from their late grandfather, who would doubtless have been extremely proud to discover this.

Fitz s old nemesis Gentleman Jim Corbett, having opted for a career on the stage, went on to appear in such productions as *The Naval Cadet* and *Byron Cashel s Profession*. He was later immortalised on film by Errol Flynn, in a Hollywood biopic of his life. He died from cancer at his home in New York s Long Island on 18 February 1933, at the age of sixty-seven.

John L Sullivan continued to live the latter part of his life with much the same vigour which had driven him in his younger, wilder days. Having been converted to temperance, he lectured on the Evils of John Barleycorn on a number of tours across the country. He died at Abingdon, Massachusetts on 2 February 1918, just a year after his old adversary.

The other major players in our story continued to lead suitably colourful lives. Wyatt Earp became a successful dealer in real estate, operating from the base in California to which he d fled following the murder of his brothers by avenging outlaws. He also prospected and mined gold, capitalising on another growth industry in

America s fledgling economy. Towards the end of his life, he also worked in Hollywood s motion picture industry — a man who d lived out the legends of the Old West, taking his place among those who could only re-enact them on the silver screen. On 13 January 1929, Wyatt Earp died in Los Angeles at the age of eighty. His house in the Hollywood Hills can be seen today, as part of the daily tours of stars homes. The scandal of the rigged fight did cast something of a temporary cloud over his reputation, especially in conjunction with reports of a compulsive gambling habit. It seems he d developed this during his days as a US deputy marshal, playing the table game of Faro with frontier gamblers. He would later be arrested at a crooked Faro game in Los Angeles. Another story has it that he was later arrested and charged following the Fitzsimmons—Sharkey fight, eventually being fined $50 for carrying an illegal pistol in his back pocket. As before, the rumours, legends and myths continue. His colleague in law-enforcement of the heavy-handed variety, Judge Roy Bean, died in 1904 and was buried in Westlawn Cemetary in Del Rio. Three years later, his son Sam was killed, and buried in the plot next to his father. There they stayed until 1964, when a relative granted permission for the graves to be moved to the grounds of the Whitehead Memorial Museum in Del Rio. William Barclay Bat Masterson, meanwhile, retired from the rough-and-tumble calling of a sharp-shooting gunman and opted instead for the comparatively tranquil life of a journalist. A New York-based sports writer, he died peacefully at his desk. Time and old age had finally caught up with the man who d survived a hundred bullets in Western shoot-outs, and protected valuable investments like Fitzsimmons as they entered the prize rings of old.

As the people in the story fall by the wayside, so too do some of the artefacts. The Dunellen property which became the Fitzsimmons family home during the last few years of the fighter s life was eventually auctioned off by the sheriff s office to help pay some of Bob s more pressing debts. Soon afterwards, a serious fire swept through the garage, gymnasium, barn and other buildings. It was later renovated and converted into a roadhouse. Named the Poplar Tree Inn, it would ultimately be raided by state troopers, investigating allegations of illegal gambling. Finally, at 4 a.m. on 7 January 1929 — twelve years after the death of its former owner — a mysterious fire consumed the entire building and its contents.

The final chapter in the remarkable story of Bob Fitzsimmons wouldn t take place until the early hours of Sunday 14 October 1999 — 102 years after he wrestled the world heavyweight prize from Jim Corbett. British-born Lennox Lewis met American Evander Holyfield in the neon-powered desert town of Las Vegas, Nevada — two impressively muscle-bound gladiators doing battle in the modern-day mausoleum of the Thomas Mack Centre. As a spectacle, it was an exact re-run of the Carson City fight of the previous century, which had taken place only a short distance away. The parallels didn t end there. The Briton, who d moved abroad as a young child, was finally meeting his long-time adversary, with nations divided on who would emerge as the ultimate warrior. When the fearsome pair clashed it was an awesome display of power, skill and technique which illuminated the desert skies above them. Lewis was cheered on by a travelling army of six thousand British fans — although there would have been no Cornish miners among the travelling throng this time.

The thirty-four-year-old London-born fighter had waited fifteen years for this moment in the world spotlight. Under the gaze of millions of TV viewers worldwide, he didn t disappoint. With his mother, Violet, providing vocal support at the ringside, echoing Rose Fitzsimmons s enthusiastic cheerleading for her husband, Lewis proved himself the better fighter, out-boxing Holyfield to take the unified crown. Thus, he became the second Briton in the sport s history who could call himself the undisputed heavyweight champion of the world, with the first resting peacefully in a Chicago cemetery.

In England, the newspapers were quick to draw comparisons between the two men. Lewis stood at an imposing six feet five and a half, carrying seventeen-and-a-half stones of heavily layered muscle on his statuesque frame. He would have towered over his 19th-century colleague, whose five foot eleven, twelve stone frame would have been more at odds with other fighters in 1999 than it was in his own era. Nevertheless, the two shared a common bond. Both had risked their lives in the hardest, most demanding pursuit known to man, and both had competed for its ulltimate prize.

Bob Fitzsimmons and Lennox Lewis would now be forever linked in history. The reign of the Cornishman as Britain s only world champion in prizefighting s uppermost echelon had, after more than a century, finally come to an end.

Postscript

History is repeating itself. Long-dead ghosts are re-awakening.

In the first few months of the twenty-first century, more than a century since the sepia-toned pictures of Fitzsimmons, Corbett and Sullivan framed an instant in world history, the story is now at last coming full-circle.

Today boxing is a billion-dollar corporate animal, which rears its head across the globe, in the form of dry-ice spectaculars and staged amid the lasers and technology of vast amphitheatres. Every single aspect of the sport is marketed, promoted, packaged as part of an all-encompassing industry. Every aspect, that is, apart from one. While the punches are harder, and the men are bigger, the spectacle of the fighting — the raw ingredient of the whole electric circus — is exactly the same as in the days of their long-dead forebears, who fought in muddy fields and filthy dust-bowls. It s this combustible element of any show which people pay to see. It can t be controlled; it can t be sanitised.

Now, more than ever, the game is ruled by a lethal cocktail of business and politics, where fees, rights and endorsements run into figures resembling telephone numbers. Moreover, the same stories come around, with an uncanny sense of detail. Moves to strip Lennox Lewis of his world heavyweight title were first raised in February 2000 by American boxing authorities, after a complaint by the flamboyant promoter Don King. King s counsel claimed Lewis had been reluctant to take on likely contenders since winning the title from Evander Holyfield in their meeting in 1999. Just as newspaper cartoons mocked Fitzsimmons for taking time away from the ring back in the nineteenth century, so the politics of the sport pressure the giant Englishman towards his next encounter, here in the twenty-first century. The strong rivalry between Britain and the States still runs as strong as in the days of Fitzsimmons s and Corbett s rivalry, with fighters battling to overcome fiercely partisan crowds in addition to their ring opponents. Where referees were once threatened at gun-point by a riverboat full of angry gamblers, now endless hearings are sparked by a controversial decision on the part of judging panels.

There is talk of controversy, decisions, appeals. There are commissions, votes, hearings. The men who risk their life in the ring are but one part of the entertainment spectacle, which pits manager against manager, promoter against promoter. The cabaret goes on twenty-four hours per day. Belts must be unified, politics must be negotiated. Where Bob Fitzsimmons once complained bitterly of being short-changed by the advent of the magical movin pitchers , those pitchers are now worth hundreds of millions of dollars, in pay-per-view rights and syndicated coverage. But the complaining still goes on. Instead of being threatened by a sheriff s gun, fighters are now faced with besuited lawyers and armies of accountants. But for the man who played such a large part in transforming illegal prizefighting into a worldwide sport, such developments are neither here nor there, as he lies peacefully in Chicago s Gracelands Cemetery. Back in his native Cornwall, schoolchildren have long urged one another to give em Fitz when engaging in sports or competition. It s a saying which means giving one s all in order to win, regardless of the odds against you. Needless to say, it was inspired by that famous Cornish son, to whom such spirit was the very stuff of life.